Pope Pius XII's Revisionism

by
Robert Faurisson

Historical Review Press
Surrey, England
2026

Historical Review Press
Reprinted 2026
Carshalton, Surrey, SM5 4JA
Bookshop: www.hrp.co.uk
E-mail: HRP@inbox.com
ISBN: 0-906879-24-8

Contents

Pope Pius XII's Revisionism

By Robert Faurisson

PREFACE

Favourable to the Allies and obligingly helpful to the Jews, Pope Pius XII was also a revisionist. It is precisely his revisionist scepticism, and not any ignorance of the facts, that explains his silence on the alleged physical extermination of the Jews, on the alleged Nazi gas chambers and on the alleged six million victims of what today is called "the Holocaust" or "the Shoah".

Favourable to the Allies, in 1940 he went so far as to act as intermediary between, on the one hand, German opponents of Hitler's regime and, on the other, France and Britain. Better still: in 1941, having to choose between Hitler and Stalin, he decided at the behest of Roosevelt, to choose Stalin. Yet "Uncle Joe" embodied the Communism which, four years previously, an encyclical had denounced as "intrinsically wrong". Thus the German army was to see its soldiers, many of whom were Roman Catholics, and their chaplains, get themselves killed in the East by American weapons supplied to the Communist regime with the Pope's secret blessing. The Germans reopened the churches closed by the Soviets but, later on, at the Nuremberg trial, they would find themselves accused - notably by a Soviet prosecutor – of religious persecution. And no one in the Vatican would protest against that criminal legal masquerade.

Obligingly helpful to the Jews, Pius XII always spoke out against racism and anti-semitism. During the war, whether is person, or through his representatives, he went to the aid of European Jews. He did so via religious, diplomatic, material and financial avenues, and through the media outlets at his direct disposal (*L'Osservatore Romano* and Vatican Radio). In his public talks he attacked the internment of large numbers of Jews in camps and ghettos, their "slow decline" (*progressivo deperimento*) as well as the "exterminating harassments" (*costrizioni sterminatrici*) to which they had been subjected. During and after the war, tribute was paid to him for his action in favour of the Jews as a whole by numerous Jewish or Zionist personalities and authorities.

Revisionist in attitude and recalling the lesson of the First World War's lies about Teutonic barbarity (children having their hands cut off, factories making products from human corpses etc.), it was with a worthy scepticism that he received the plethora of cacophonous stories of Nazi death-works. Before imputing the alleged crimes to Adolf Hitler, whom he abhorred, he wanted to have confirmations and precise information. He was not supplied with these and was, at times, told that the obvious needed no proving. Then, rightly, he decided to keep quiet about things that were merely the stuff of unfounded rumours.

His scepticism in this regard was like that of the wartime Allied leaders, albeit more clear-cut. The latter, in their anti-Nazi diatribes, were assuredly scathing about the "extermination" of the Jews but with the rhetorical bluster of war speeches and solely and conventional sense, so that by "extermination" they meant excesses, maltreatment, mass executions, famine. In August 1943 they had almost gone further and spoke of "gas chambers" but the Foreign Office in London and the State Department in Washington, inundated with Jewish propaganda, decided by mutual agreement that there was "insufficient evidence" for them to talk about German execution gas chambers (August 29, 1943). In the same spirit during and after the war, Churchill, Eisenhower and de Gaulle avoided mentioning the alleged gas chambers or gas vans in either their speeches or their memoirs.

Today, a certain Jewish or Zionist propaganda lays a blanket of blame on Pius XII, Roosevelt, Churchill, Stalin, the International Committee of the Red Cross, various resistance movements, the countries that stayed neutral and just about the whole universe. All find themselves rebuked for their indifference or silence with respect to the "little nation that has suffered so much". Their descendants or successors must publicly express penance (*techouva*) and pay up.

If truth be told, Pope Pius X has some defenders, and, amongst them, some Jews. For these people, if the Pope kept quiet about the awful fate of the Jews, it was "because he didn't know". Besides, the allied officials, they add, knew no more about it either, hence their own silence, their inaction, their refusal to bomb Auschwitz. The explanation is pitiful. It rests on speculation alone. It aggravates the case of those whom it seeks to defend: it makes deaf, blind and ignorant men of them.

If, for three or for years running, a physical extermination of such dimensions had been perpetrated with such horrible means as those gigantic chemical slaughterhouses, in the very heart of Europe (a Europe that was largely transparent, whatever else we have been told), and if the results had been the demise of six million people (the equivalent of the population of Switzerland), people would have been aware of it and traces of the crime would abound. In fact, not a trace has yet been found, not one document pertaining to it has been discovered, and for a good reason. The "Wannsee" minutes attest to the contrary of an extermination policy for they provide for the "freeing" (*Freilassung*) of the Jews at the end of the war and the creation of the Jewish entity somewhere outside Europe. On the other hand, from 1945, this alleged planned massacre produced millions of European Jews dubbing themselves "living witnesses to the genocide", "survivors" or "miraculous escapees". For anyone willing to reflect on it, these people constitute, quite unwillingly, rather an impressive body of "living proof" of the fact that there was, in reality, neither "Holocaust" nor "Shoah".

For the devotees of the "Shoah" religion, the magical gas chamber is everything, permitting everything (Louis-Ferdinand Céline's words in 1950). This myth is the sword and shield of Israel. It authorises exorbitant power, privileges, pressure, extortion and blackmail. "Auschwitz" is wielded as a "moral cudgel" (Martin Walser in 1998). The first victim is defeated Germany; the second is an insulted Christendom and the third is the Arabo-Moslem world slated for constant humiliation.

Over the span of three decades Pope Pius XII's successors tried to offer some resistance to the rising flood of Jewish demands and recriminations grounded in the great lie. But both John XXIII and Paul VI had to yield step by step. As for John Paul II, who acceded to the papacy in 1978, his attempts at resistance lasted eleven years. In 1989, during the affair of the Carmelite nuns and their cross at Auschwitz, in the course of which he was to lay down his arms, he evoked, in a message to the Polish Episcopal conference, the "extermination of the Jews" in the "gas chambers". In 1990 he repeated the gesture with a like remark before a group of Poles at an audience in the Vatican. In 1992 he condemned historical revisionism. In 1993 he recognised the State of Israel. In 1998, he spoke out in so many words, against the Shoah, that cruel plan to exterminate a people – "a plan to which millions of our Jewish brothers and sisters fell victim". In so behaving, he condemned Pius XII, for whom a process of beatification was thus rendered impossible. And all that to the great satisfaction of the Jews who, as is well known, were demanding that a halt be put to that process.

For those who wish to do so, the only way to rehabilitate the memory of the "maligned Pope" is to speak the language of verifiable truth, historical exactitude or, quite simply, the facts.

At the same time they will happen to be defending the victims, who today number in their billions, of the "hoax of the twentieth century" (Arthur Robert Butz).

Pope Pius XII's Revisionism

[May 8, 2006]

Although wholly won over to the Allied cause and resolutely opposed to racism and anti-semitism, Pope Pius XII still did not lend credence to all the rumours that were put about, during and after the Second World War, on the subject of atrocities imputed to the Third Reich.

People readily speak of his "silence" on what today is by the general consensus called the "Holocaust" or the "Shoah" (that is essentially, the alleged "extermination of the Jews" in the alleged "Nazi gas chambers" and the alleged "six million Jewish victims"). Some find fault with the Pope for having kept quiet about those atrocities, which are presented as real; others, believing they are coming to his aid, explain that, if the sovereign pontiff had broken his silence to denounce publicly such an abomination, he would have aroused the fury of Hitler, and thus, it is said, would have worsened the plight of the Jews.

The argument is far from convincing.

There is no doubt that on many occasions (such as, notably, in May 1940, when speaking on the subject of Poland defeated by Germany and the Soviet Union) Pope Pius XII would have wished to pronounce "fiery words" and that he abstained from doing so with a view to sparing the victims a possible harshening of conditions. But the crime of the "Shoah", as it is complacently described to us, is so monstrous that one can hardly conceive how it might have been made any worse. To begin with, no religious or moral authority could have passed over it in silence for any imaginable consideration of propriety. However, on June 4, 1944, when all the Allied troops entered Rome, the Pope, who gave them a warm welcome, continued to keep quiet on the matter. With the end of the war in Europe on May 8, 1945, Pope Pius XII persisted in his silence. On June 2 of that year he gave a pitiless talk before the College of Cardinals against National Socialism and Hitler; he condemned their "most exquisite scientific methods to torture or eliminate people who were often innocent"; he spoke out against the use of prisons and concentration camps, particularly that of Dachau where Christian believers and priests had been interned alongside political detainees, but he had not a word to say about any process of physical extermination of the Jews or the use of execution gas chambers. On that subject he was to remain quiet until his death in 1958. Why the stubborn silence?

Such muteness is all the more intriguing as, from 1939 to 1945, far from remaining impartial with regard to the belligerents, the Pope showed himself to be resolutely favourable to the cause of the Allies and hostile to the Axis forces. He made no mystery of his sympathy for Poland, France, Britain and the United States. Of course, he liked the Italian people and the German people but bemoaned their having Mussolini and Hitler for leaders. Fascism repelled him whilst National Socialism and Communism filled him with horror and fear. For as long as Stalin and Hitler made common cause, that is, from August 23, 1939 (the signing of the Germano-Soviet pact) to June 22, 1941 (Germany's launching of war against the Soviet Union), he deemed the two dictators equally detestable. But when Joseph Stalin found himself in the Allies' camp and Franklin Roosevelt, keen to come to the aid of "Uncle Joe", requested of the Pope an intervention in line with that intent (in the form of words to be addressed to American Catholics), Pius XII then had, in a certain way, to choose between Hitler and Stalin. As will be seen further on, he chose Stalin. That choice serves to show how dear the Allied cause was to him.

His silence on the "Holocaust" of the Jews becomes still less comprehensible when one considers his repulsion for anti-semitism and (he impressive number, throughout the war and afterwards, of his direct and indirect interventions in favour of the Jews.

For this puzzling silence of Pius XII there is, as we shall see, but one explanation: to the end of his life, the Pope treated the story of the "Nazi gas chambers", the "genocide of the Jews" and the "six million Jewish victims" as though he saw in it one and the same rumour, an exaggeration, an invention of war propaganda. All told, his attitude in this respect was that of a revisionist.

He was a revisionist in the manner of Winston Churchill, Charles de Gaulle; Dwight Eisenhower and a fair number of other eminent officials of the Allied camp or the neutral countries who, either during or after the war; whilst showing both aversion for National Socialism and sympathy for the Jews, still refused to accept the reality of the "Holocaust" and, for instance, never wrote or uttered the fatal words "gas chamber(s) [1]*".*

Eisenhower's Crusade in Europe (1948), W. Churchill's six-volume The Second World War (1948-1954), and Charles de Gaulle's *Mémoires de Guerre* (1954-1959) constitute a mass of over 7,000 pages written after the conflict; however, to take them as an example, no trace of the gas chambers is to be found therein. Thus from the point of view of those three prominent witnesses of the Second World War, the Nazi "gas chambers" were less than a detail and, for them, everything had gone on as if those chemical slaughterhouses did not exist. Likewise, Pius XII spoke of them neither expressly nor in the allusive style proper to the Vatican; he did not do so, I repeat, either during the war or afterwards.

His "silence" concerned that which is disputed by the revisionists, i.e. the "genocide of the Jews", the "Nazi gas chambers", the "extermination camps" (this last expression being a creation of Allied propaganda) and the "six million Jewish victims". For the remainder, i.e. the hardships unquestionably endured by the Jews, the discriminatory measures that they had to suffer, the deportations, the living conditions in the concentration camps, far from maintaining any silence, Pius XII, already in the middle of the war, spoke out on those realities and, especially, with greater effectiveness than anyone else in the world, he acted in defence of the Jews. He did so both personally and through the offices of his representatives. Also, after the war, there were Jews, and not the humblest of that folk, who paid him resounding tribute. Still today, some Jews defend the late Pope against those who, abusively, take him to task for his "silence" on the travails of the people of Israel when they are not, equally unjustly, decrying his alleged "silence" on the hardships of the Serbs or the Poles.

HE SPOKE OUT AGAINST THE VERITABLE EXCESSES AND KEPT QUIET ON THE SUBJECT OF UNSUBSTANTIATED HORRORS

Pope Pius XII condemned racism, anti-semitism, the lot reserved for the Jews by the Germans, the arrest of innocent civilians, the deportations, the concentration or forced labour camps and what he termed either the "slow decline" (*progressivo deperimento*) or the "exterminating harassments" (*costrizioni sterminatrici*) to which some persons in those camps were at times subjected because of their nationality alone (Polish, for instance) or race (Jewish, for instance).

In this respect, he did not name the Poles and the Jews but he clearly designated them. No one was mistaken about that. The Germans saw in this a breaching of the impartiality to which the Vatican ought to keep. In its article on Pius XII, *The Encyclopedia of the Holocaust* (1990) states: "The reference to Jews was clear but not explicit" but one may just as well judge that "the reference to the Jews was not explicit but clear".

Pius XII would not have failed to go still further and speak out about the reality of a "genocide" and of "gas chambers" (or "gas vans") had he been supplied with proof thereof. *He asked for that proof but was unable to get it.* There were even occasions where those who informed him on the matter refused to substantiate the claims, alleging that the obvious needed no proving. Thus the Pope attacked excesses that seemed to him to be real but would not condemn atrocities that appeared doubtless too much like the propaganda lies and baseless rumours of the First World War. His generation (he was thirty-eight years old in 1914) had been marked by the disclosure, shortly after the end of that conflict, by the Allies themselves of the lies that they acknowledged having invented on the score of Teutonic barbarism whilst, at its end, the German propaganda with its Belgian atrocity stories had not lagged far behind. He immediately suspected that certain accounts of Nazi horrors being passed on to him by Jewish or Allied agencies might well be nothing but classic exaggerations of war propaganda. After all, did not the tales of the "death factories" where the Germans were methodically killing Jews and turning them into soap, fertiliser and various other products resemble, like peas in a pod, the stories of the "corpse factories" of the previous war? Pius XII was able to distinguish the true tragedies from unproved abominations. He alerted the world to the former and had the good sense to keep quiet about the latter. In point of fact he reasoned, concluded and acted as a revisionist. His "silence" concerned exclusively horrors which, because they seemed to him to be possible inventions of war propaganda, called for no denunciation on his part. As a man of wisdom and conscience, he shrank at bringing a defamatory charge against the German people and so slandering his neighbour. His silence was at first that of a spirit for whom "knowledge without conscience is but the ruin of the soul"; then, the silence in question was that of the highest authority in the Church, for which prudence is a cardinal virtue. His case could be summed up, *here*, in three Latin words: *Scientia, Conscientia, Prudentia.* but as will be seen further on, Pius XII did happen at times to sin through imprudence, through a lack of impartiality, through political ruse, and there it was at the expense of Hitler and Mussolini, the future vanquished, and not at the expense of Churchill, Roosevelt and Stalin, the future victors.

HIS PARTIALITY FOR THE JEWS AND THE ALLIES

His direct or indirect action in favour of the Jews was considerable. In all Europe (particularly in France in the summer of 1942) and even elsewhere in the world, through the offices of his "ministers", nuncios, apostolic envoys, cardinals, archbishops and bishops, along with the superiors of monasteries and convents, he steadily pursued a policy of protecting the sons and daughters of Israel. For the defence of the Jews, he went so far as in take covert initiatives which, as will be seen later, were in violation of certain laws and rules. The aversion that he harboured towards Hitler had the effect of leading him to imprudence, as will be demonstrated below. It is nonsense to speak of a collusion on his part with Hitler or even with Mussolini. Besides, the latter declared publicly that "the Vatican is a chronic case of appendicitis for Italy" whilst other Fascists spoke of "cancer". On June 30, 1944, when Marshal Pétain was still in power in France, with Léon Bérard representing him at the Holy See, Pius XII received General de Gaulle under the protocol reserved for heads of state. It was with open arms that he received also the official visits of officers' and soldiers' delegations from the British, American and Canadian forces, including those amongst them who, by atrocious bombing raids, had killed many civilians. Roberto Farinacci was not the only Fascist to state his indignation at the Pope's taking of sides, to be outraged by his refusal to support the Italians who went to fight on the Eastern front against "atheistic Communism" and disgusted at his silence on the dissection of Europe decided at the Yalta conference (February 4-11,1945). Germans and Italians were often indignant at the Pope's silence or "silences". *L'Osservatore Romano* and Vatican Radio were their *bêtes noires.* On all of these points one may consult the work by Owen Chadwick, *Britain and the Vatican, during the Second World War* (Cambridge University Press, London, 1986;

(p. 107, 109, 186, 306-307). In general, any historian who wonders about what it is now customary to call "Pius XII's silence" ought to go over all of the Pope's silences before, during and after the war; then he would likely realise that, if the Pope can be criticised for having said or done nothing, it would rather be in regard to the moments where the victors, sure of their right to do whatever they wanted, piled up an unheard-of score of excesses of all kinds to the detriment of the vanquished: gigantic deportations, summary executions, bloody "purges", pillaging such as the world had never seen, tribunals at which, with the fighting over, the winner put the loser on trial holding him at his mercy and sentencing him to the gallows at the end of a judicial masquerade. In France, in 1944-1945, voices like that of father Panici, canon Desgranges or other clerics who had previously spoken out in favour of the Jews and who were now indignant at the horrors of the "Purge" were extremely rare; practically no one dared then confront the all-powerful Communist Party, the Jews or Charles de Gaulle himself and voice indignation at their excesses (including the spectacle of "collaborationist" women paraded through the streets after having their heads shaved). In Germany, a few churchmen who, during the war, had made themselves known by way of their intercessions on behalf of the Jews ended up being disturbed at the repression exerted by the Allies. It does not appear that the Pope, if ever he did break his silence at those moments, took much action. The stories that are peddled about the help given by the Vatican to "Nazis" on the run are to a large degree just as imaginary as the yarns spun around the ODESSA network.

JEWISH GRATITUDE TOWARDS PIUS XII

During and after the war Pius XII received solid tribute from top-ranking Jewish personalities for his action in favour of the Jews at the time of all their perils. Names that may be cited, along with a good many others, are those of Israel (or Israele) Anton Zoller (1881-1956), alias Italo Zolli, chief rabbi of Rome, and Golda Meir, foreign secretary of the Jewish State (she would later serve as its Prime Minister).

Italo Zolli, on February 13, 1945, the day of his and his wife's conversion to the Catholic religion (their daughter was to convert as well later on), was keen to be baptised Eugenio, the Christian name of Pius XII (Eugenio Pacelli), whilst his wife chose the name Eugenia. Eugenia Zolli was ever disposed to point out that journalists were mistaken in ascribing in ascribing conversion to his gratitude towards Pius XII. It arose from other motives indeed, but his gratitude was no less certain in regard to a Pope who had done so much for the Jews and for many non-Jews as well [2].

Pinchas Lapide (1922-1997) devoted an entire part of his life to the defence of Pius XII. Israeli consul general in Milan well after the war, he rose up against the attacks on the sovereign pontiff made by an atheist like Albert Camus or a Catholic like François Mauriac and, especially, by a German Protestant, Rolf Hochhuth. In 1963, Hochhuth brought out a lengthy indictment of the late Pope that he produced in the form of a stage play entitled *Der Stellvertreter* (known in English translation as *The Deputy or The Representative*). An orthodox Jewish academic specialising in New Testament studies, P. Lapide in 1967 published a book entitled, in its English version, *Three Popes and the Jews: Pope Pius XII Did not Remain Silent* (Hawthorn Books, New York), in which he stated the estimate, drawn from Ins own experience and his research in the archives at Yad Vashem, that the Catholic Church had saved at least 700,000 but, more likely, 860,000 Jews "from certain death at the hands of the Nazis".

Some Jewish specialists of the "Holocaust" like Martin Gilbert or Richard Breitman have also on occasion taken up the defence of the wartime pontiff but the most active of all seems, still today, to be rabbi David G. Dalin, associate professor at the Jewish Theological Seminary of New York. The author of a study entitled "A Righteous Gentile: Pope Pius X11 and the Jews" [3], he has produced numerous articles and given interviews and lectures on the subject in various languages and in several countries. In a piece entitled "Pius XII and the Jews" (*Weekly Standard*, New York, February 26, 2001), he listed the names of Jewish personalities who, amongst a good number of others, had wished to show their gratitude to that Pope: Albert Einstein already in 1940, Chaïm Weizmann, Moshe Sharett, Golda Meir, Isaac Herzog (who was chief rabbi of Israel), Leon Kubowitzky (Secretary General of the World Jewish Congress on the occasion, in September 1945, of that organisation's donation of $20,000 to Vatican charities) and Elio Toaff, chief rabbi of Rome. In 1955, the Union of Italian Jewish Communities proclaimed April 17 a "'Day of Gratitude' for the Pope's wartime assistance in defying the Nazis". On May 26 of the same year, conductor Paul Kletzki and the Israeli Philharmonic Orchestra, flew to Rome for a state-sponsored visit during which they performed Beethoven's Seventh Symphony before the pontiff in the Vatican's Consistory Hall, "to express the State of Israel's enduring gratitude for the help that the Pope and the Catholic Church had given to the Jewish people persecuted by the Nazis during the Holocaust". A poignant detail: D.G. Dalin calls historians like John Cornwell "revisionists" for accusing the Pope of having yielded too much to Hitler (Cornwell is the author of *Hitler's Pope: The Secret History of Pius XII*, Viking, New York, 1999); for Dalin, in effect, "revisionist" writers are those who deny the obvious. It may be said in passing that Cornwell's book does not live up to its title: not a trace is to be found in the text of any "secret history" and the expression "Hitler's Pope" seems to be there merely to get the bookshop browser's attention and the Lobby's favour; the publishers of the French translation preferred the title *Le Pape et Hitler* which, in its banality, happens to match up better with the book's contents and lack of any real or truly new substance.

More complete information on the actions and the publications of Pius XII's three main Jewish defenders can be found through an internet search engine - "Google", for example - by entering the names "Eugenio Zolli", "Pinchas Lapide" and "David G. Dalin".

THE SOUND SCEPTICISM OF PIUS XII, THE ALLIES AND THE NEUTRALS

The senior Allied leaders gave free rein to their own war propaganda offices, journalists and judicial henchmen as far as atrocity stories were concerned but, for their own part, they avoided giving endorsement to such rumours. One and the same reserve was maintained first at the London Foreign Office, then at the State Department in Washington, both of which were flooded with alleged "intelligence" on the enemy's atrocities and incessantly pressed on the subject by Jewish groups or agencies. Upon verification, the most alarming items of "intelligence" showed themselves to be nothing but groundless rumours that could be ascribed above all to various Jews who "tended to exaggerate the German atrocities in order to stoke us up [4]". As for the heads of the International Committee of the Red Cross, they did not depart from the cautious line followed by the Allies,

They tried as much as the Foreign Office or the State Department to confirm the rumours circulating about the Nazi gas chambers and wound up having to conclude there was insufficient evidence; otherwise they would not have failed to speak of them, during the war, as a horrible reality. Roosevelt personally maintained silence on this question even when, from November 1944, the War Refugee Board, directly linked to the White House and supported by the combative Jew Henry Morgenthau Jr, secretary of the Treasury, was nonetheless putting about the account, an absurd one at that, carried by what has been called the "Auschwitz Protocols" or the "War Refugee Board Report".

The senior British officials could not believe in the alleged homicidal gassings, for their deciphering specialists had managed to break the codes used by the Germans in their secret communications, and London's services in charge of reading the countless intercepted messages found no mention therein of such gassings: "There were no references in the decrypts to gassing [5]". How, for example, could the Foreign Office heads have lent credence to atrocity stories identical or similar to those which were being fabricated to order within their very own ministry by a bureau discreetly named "Political Warfare Executive"? For example, during a campaign of false news addressed to the Arab world, where the Germans enjoyed great prestige, the PWE had made up and diffused the following information: 1) In the occupied Tripoli region, the Germans turned mosques into brothels; 2) they were lacking in textiles to such a point that they had the Moslem dead dug up from their graves in order to take their burial shrouds and send them to carpet factories in Germany; 3) on entering Tunis, the Allied troops had discovered in the German army's storehouses the remains of children rendered into meat, the cuts of which were labelled pork "rations" [6].

Eduard Benes, who in London headed the Czechoslovak government in exile, had some *lengthy* tasks of verification carried out concerning the rumours of the Jews' being exterminated and concluded that, contrary to what the Jew Gerhart Riegner led others to believe, the Germans had no plan aiming at such an extermination; according to Benes Jews continued to be left at liberty where they dwelt and moved about unhindered; certainly, with defeat approaching, the Nazis were becoming, said he, more oppressive but they behaved in a like way with the other fringe elements of the population and no particular treatment seemed to be reserved to the

Jews [7]. But, in point of fact, had not Riegner, in his all-too-famous telegram of August 10, 1942, added a qualifying statement to the news of a plan to exterminate the Jews, words that too many "Holocaust" historians have hastened to forget? Had he not written: "We transmit this information with all the necessary reservation, as exactitude cannot be confirmed by us [8]"?

In reply to the mythomaniacal Pole Jan Karski, the American Jew Felix Frankfurter, a Supreme Court Justice, simply said: "I can't believe you [9]".

In France, as late as in January 1945, the public prosecutor Reboul, although quite bent on having the author Robert Brasillach sentenced to death, would mention only "the exceptionally severe camps, in Poland".

SERIOUS JEWISH INFORMATION
ON THE REAL FATE OF THE JEWS

We are repeatedly told today that during the war, information on the Jews' fate was not wanting. What we are supposed to understand by this is that it was a deadly fate, with the said information bearing that out. In reality, no such thing. The intelligence was contradictory, if not cacophonous. Some of it was alarming and, in general, obviously exaggerated and quite imprecise whilst some was precise and, by comparison, rather reassuring, being garnered from good sources. Hence the widespread scepticism (or the revisionism) that reigned at the Vatican and elsewhere amongst those who received, amidst a flood of dishevelled accounts, certain orderly and detailed ones: it was easy for them, by way of simple contrast, to tell the likely from the unlikely, if not the true from the false. On the subject of serious information, we may confine ourselves to the case of father Marie-Benoît, "padre to the Jews", and to that of the Zionist bulletin *Shem* (Hebrew word meaning "The Name" or designating "the legendary ancestor of the Semites, the first of the Hebrews").

To remain with the Vatican itself, if there was a man, close to Pius XII, who could have believed the rumours of the Jews' physical extermination, it was he who has often been called "padre to the Jews". The French Capuchin monk Pierre Peteul, in his vocation father Marie-Benoît or padre Maria-Benedetto, maintained the closest relations with the extremely rich American Jewish Joint Distribution Committee ("the Joint") as well as with the Jewish communities in France, Italy and elsewhere. He had thousands of Italian Jews supplied with false documents. Michael Phayer, in his book otherwise quite hostile to Pius XII, calls father Marie-Benoît "the outstanding French Franciscan rescuer [10]".

Father Marie-Benoît took in a mass of information obtained from Jewish sources and forwarded it to the Pope. At a private audience of July 1,1, 1943 he gave Pius XII a document entitled "Information on the Camps of Upper Silesia", in which it was reported that in those camps (Auschwitz-Birkenau was mentioned) "morale among the deportees is generally good, and they are hopeful as to their future [11]". As early as in 1948 the French author Maurice Bardèche produced long extracts of this text, which had been reproduced in the clandestine issue n° 8 of *Shem* dated July 1944 [12].

Shem, "journal of Hebraic action", had its offices at 6, rue Vavin in the sixth arrondissement in Paris. Those in charge were Georges Blumberg, Ammi-Horon, E. Sinko and Charles Driard. The first issue (111 pages) bore the date May 1939 (its cover indicates June 1939). It was ultra-Zionist In inspiration: the Jews must reconquer Palestine; the enemies were the British and the Arabs; support must be given to the *Irgun Zvaï Leumi*, which was the Jewish peoples national military organisation. One may note, in passing, that the mythical figure of "six million" made an appearance here In 1939; it was a matter, in effect, of "the nearly six million Jews of the East being threatened with the same fate as their brethren in the Reich" (p. 103). During the German occupation the journal went underground. Bardèche said that it was "the only clandestine resistance organ giving [in French] any precise information on the deportation camps". The information in question is surprising in its diversity and gives the impression of resulting from very extensive and serious inquiries. For such or such camp, living conditions are described as "catastrophic" but, for the region that interests us here and which, according to the legend, was host to the most enormous "extermination camp" of all time, that of Auschwitz-Birkenau, the report reads as follows:

> Life in these camps is bearable, given the proximity of camps for non-Jewish workers and, in some places, the participation of inmates from camps of either type in work such as road, bridge and house building. It is craftsmen, preferably, who are accepted for these jobs. Morale among the deportees is generally good, and they are hopeful as to their future [13].

The same text is reproduced in *Actes et documents du Saint-Siège relatifs à la Seconde Guerre Mondiale (ADSS)*, Libreria Editrice Vaticana, 1965-1982, vol. 9: "Le Saint-Siège et les victimes de la guerre (janvier-décembre 1943)", 1975, pages 42 and 396 (note). There, again according to Bardèche, the following details on Jewish children can be read; judging by what is I known from other sources, they seem accurate:

> A very large number of newborns and infants under the age of two, of Jewish parents, are housed in Berlin proper and in the surrounding region in various crèches and nurseries. They are always taken there by the DRK (German Red Cross) and the NSVW (German Social Organisation) as children of persons who have been made homeless or killed in the aerial bombardments, together with children from the rest of the population, and are generally admitted as such amongst the other orphans [14].

That is just what it says: it is a question here of Jewish orphans being treated on an equal footing with the German orphans by the German Red Cross and the NSVW, i.e. the *Nationalsozialistische Volkswohlfahrt*, the National Socialist public assistance organisation. Today we possess a number of documents, photographs and witnesses' statements attesting to the fact that, contrary to what is put about in "Holocaust" propaganda, the German authorities, to the extent that the horrors of war allowed, treated Jewish children humanely. Whence, more than fifty years after the war, all the Jewish septuagenarians who returned from the camps and ghettos then and who introduce themselves as "miraculous survivors" now.

If, during and after the war, so many high officials failed to breathe a word of the "gas chambers" and "gas vans", it was because they knew where they stood in respect to the quality of information being circulated by their own propaganda agencies. They refused to draw from the gutter and spread the muck. The sovereign pontiff behaved in the same way. He did not consent to take part in what deserves to be called the anti-German lie bazaar.

THE ANTI-GERMAN LIE BAZAAR

Quite a number of examples could be given of similar reluctance to accept at face value stories rich in imprecise precision, like those that were peddled with the war going on at fever pitch, or that the media diffuse still today in the greatest confusion and with a success to match their impudence.

At that time there was a steady flow of unverified testimonies about gas chambers, gas vans, railway carriages turned into chemical slaughterhouses, vacuum chambers..., and they are persistently churned out in our own day and age as well; on November 22, 1941, in Boston, rabbi Joshua Loth Liebman declared to a gathering of young Zionists that one day indemnities and a place in Palestine would have to be requested in reparation for the death of the millions of Jews killed, notably, in "refrigerated cars [15]". There was talk then and there is still talk today of killings by electricity, by quicklime, by intravenous injection of air or cyanide, by insecticide, hydrogen cyanide, carbon monoxide or dioxide, by the emissions from a tank or submarine engine, by boiling water or steam (the first official version for Treblinka, UN related in Nuremberg document PS-3311, of which the tribunal took "judicial notice"). There was a fondness for stories, whether of Jewish fat used to produce bars of soap or of the bones of Jews made into fertiliser and, still in the present day, there are to be found in some Jewish cemeteries, one in Nice for example, urns supposedly containing "Jewish soap". There was also talk of human skin transformed into lampshades or book-bindings whereas the skins in question, once examined, turned out to be morocco (goatskin). The "Nazis" had, it was said, forced a prisoner to imitate a dog churned in its kennel, barking at passers-by and keenly plunging his maw into the food bowl [16]. And what can one say of the stories of dogs trained to bite Jews in their private parts or to force themselves on Jewesses? What to make of the caged bear and eagle in Buchenwald, to which the Germans each day threw a live Jew, the bear tearing said Jew to pieces and the eagle feasting on his bones? Let us take care not to forget the hangings of inmates in bunches on Christmas trees, the machines, each one more ingenious than the rest, for liquidating the Jews, the Jewish babies shoved *alive* into the crematory ovens, the Hitler Youth using Jewish babies for target practice, the SS man throwing babies in the air and shooting them, to the applause of his daughter, who shouted for more. On the score of medical experiments, the sources were and are inexhaustible: we are told that Dr Mengele, for instance, kept on the wall of his laboratory "several dozen human eyes pinned up like a butterfly collection [17]"; sometimes the children whom this "Angel of Death" had fun "treating" returned to their quarters only after becoming "hardly recognisable", for they were henceforth "stitched together back to back like Siamese twins [18]"; "with a passion for the study of mutations [Mengele] burns the dark eyes of Gypsies with acid to find out whether they turn blue [19]". Had not an atomic bomb test near Auschwitz "eradicated almost instantaneously" 20,000 Jews? At the Nuremberg trial a festival of fakes of every sort, the American prosecutor Jackson, in all seriousness, questioned Albert Speer on this last point on June 21, 1946 [20]. One may recall here the Dreyfusard Charles Peguy's considerations on testimonies for history:

> However, God knows, says [Clio, the muse of history], that there is no-where so much lying as in testimony, (because then it becomes historical), and that witnesses lie all the more when their testimony is most solemn [21].

During the war, heads of Zionist organisations poured out a Niagara of inventions of that ilk from Berne or Geneva in the direction of the Vatican and the Allies. It was what today's accusers of Pius XII call "the information that the Pope did not want to take into account". One of the agencies regularly manufacturing such items was located in Bratislava, Slovakia. There Michael Dov Weissmandel, a rabbi of Hungarian origin, was in charge; it is to him that we have owed, since May 1944, the now sacrosanct figure of the Six Million Jews killed by the Nazis and the outlandish story of the Auschwitz escapees, the all too famous Rudolf Vrba (who died on March 27, 2006) amongst them. In 1985, at the first trial of the German-Canadian revisionist Ernst Zündel, witness Vrba was to collapse under cross-examination carried out, with my assistance, by barrister Douglas Christie: battle-weary, Vrba the mythomaniac ended up admitting that, in his account of Auschwitz, he had used *"licentia poetarum"* (sic). That episode was not to stop him from swaggering forth once again, ten years later, in a documentary which will be mentioned further on, or from recycling his lies as recently as in 2001 in a new version of his "account" (sic, previously known as *I Cannot Forgive*) entitled *I Escaped from Auschwitz* (Barricade Books - Fort Lee, New Jersey, 2002). A swindler does not mend his ways: he stays a swindler till the end of his existence. R. Vrba became one of the leading false witnesses in the campaign mounted against Pius XII.

ACCOUNTS OF ATROCITIES BUT NO EVIDENCE

The Vatican had also sought to verify the reality of some of those horrors and had found no evidence. In this instance, a deplorable kind of reasoning, destined to meet with the most resounding success after the war and up until today, was inaugurated by Casimir Papée, Poland's ambassador to the Holy See. He resorted to a type of subterfuge often practised by slanderers and the shiftless: to the Vatican authorities who were demanding proof he replied curtly that "there was sufficient proof and, besides, when something becomes notorious, proof is not required [22]". The judges at the International Military Tribunal at Nuremberg were to talk no differently in 1945 when decreeing: "The Tribunal shall not be bound by technical rules of evidence [...], The Tribunal shall not require proof of facts of common knowledge but shall take judicial notice thereof (articles 19 and 21 of their tribunal's charter, written by... the tribunal itself).

A POPE WHO WAS PARTICULARLY
HELPFUL TO THE JEWS

There and nowhere else is the silence of Pius XII. However, with some rare exceptions, his denigrators seek to maintain ambiguity. In general they would have people believe that they find fault with the accused for his silence in the face of *all the hardships* inflicted on the Jews by the Germans. We may look at an example taken from the French monthly *L'Histoire*, published under the supervision, in particular, of Michel Winock and Jean-Noël Jeanneney. The introductory note for an article on "Pie XII, Hitler et les Juifs" reads that the Pope "refused to condemn the persecution of the Jews during the Second World War [23]". A brazen lie. In reality, the Pope's silence essentially concerned what, according to the revisionists, simply did not and could not exist. That silence was urged on Pius XII by a circumspection of revisionist nature. But none of the accusers dare set forth the grounds for their thinking or clearly articulate their grievances. None of them cries out as, after all, they clearly should, that "Pius XII refused to condemn the genocide of the Jews and the Nazi gas chambers for, in his own way, he was a Holocaust denier". Such is one of the great prohibition's effects. There is the fear of violating the taboo (here, the taboo of taboos) by uttering the word that creates it. To disclose that Pius XII had a revisionist's reflex would, for his accusers, amount to bringing grist to the mill of those whom they call the "negationists". So it is that all too many prosecutors to be seen parading their unlikely indictments before the court of history whilst at their end the Pope's defenders, themselves as well in dread the taboo and fearing the accusation of anti-semitism, have acquired the unfortunate habit of creating a diversion: they take up the defence of the accused on a terrain where he has no need at all of a lawyer, for here it an "open and shut" case. What need is there to defend the wartime Pope, against the accusation of anti-semitism? A thousand pieces of evidence, a thousand documents, a thousand actions prove that Pius XII, during the war just as before it, showed in word and deed that he condemned anti semitism and that he sought either to prevent any persecution of racialist character or to heal the possible effects thereof. For his part, did not Louis Ferdinand Céline denounce in the Roman Catholic Church what he called "the great race-mixer"?

A POPE WHO WAS ALSO TOUCHED BY OTHER SORROWS THAN THOSE OF THE JEWS

Deeply hostile to anti-semitism, the Pope, however, was not to give privileged status to the Jews' sufferings. Why would he have done so? Because those sufferings made more noise? Because the press of the whole Western World was turning itself into their echo chamber? The Poles had their share of torments inflicted on the war's defeated. The European populations, particularly in Germany, were experiencing the living nightmare of bombing raids that targeted civilians. Hostages were being taken in all circles of society. Soldiers faced death and maiming on all the many battlefields. Widows and orphans would number in the millions, famines and epidemics would strike everywhere. But it must be acknowledged that the Jews do not care to see their hardships compared to those of others: theirs are decreed "incomparable", "unique", "unspeakable" and would seem to be singled out from all the rest as much by their quality, which was, supposedly, horrific, as by their quantity, which, supposedly, was enormous. If certain specific atrocities like the mass-killing of Jews in gas chambers had occurred, the Pope would assuredly have considered the sufferings inflicted on the Jews as specially horrific and appalling; but, for him, what with the account of those atrocities being apparently unaccompanied by evidence, it was not fitting to give special status to the Jews' suffering by evoking abominations that were perhaps imaginary. Here one encounters an example of what must indeed be called Pius XII's revisionism, a natural, spontaneous, rare kind of revisionism that has the effect of fostering sensitivity to one's neighbour's plight, free of any racial or religious criterion. There is no "chosen people", not even for suffering.

To tell the truth, the Pope may after all have made a distinction between Jews of the Jewish religion and those of the Catholic. He showed, it seems, more solicitude for the latter than for the former. This is explainable. It is only human for a shepherd to be most concerned with his own flock but, especially, Catholics of Jewish origin, when persecuted for their ethnicity, found themselves particularly isolated and vulnerable. Their original community generally rejected them, considering them as renegades. These converts to Catholicism could not, when hardship came, benefit from the rich subsidies of the international or national Jewish organisations. It must be recalled that, for the whole duration of the war, with the agreement of the Third Reich authorities, a body like "the Joint", already mentioned, distributed in Europe, even in the camps and the ghettos, considerable sums in US dollars to persons ill or associations authorised by the Germans to come to the aid of the Jews. The Vatican archives show that, in such circumstances, "the Holy See began with the fate of baptised Jews, for this group was in very great need since relief organisations were often unaware of them [24]". On February 28, 1941. Mgr Innitzer, Archbishop of Vienna, in a letter to the Vatican,

reiterated his great disappointment that baptised Jews were being forgotten and the unfortunate contrast with the [Protestant] Quakers, the [Protestant] Swedish mission, and Jewish organisations. Catholics of Jewish origin had been "terribly deceived [sic: doubtless an error on the part of an English translator; the correct word is *disappointed* - translator's note]" In the eyes of their Jewish co-religionists, they were apostates and renegades; their conversion meant that all financial assistance came to an end [25].

FAVOURABLE TO THE ALLIES' CAUSE

Emotional, as quick to show enthusiasm as to shed tears, compassionate, circumspect like a diplomat but sometimes bold to the point of rashness, endowed with a Latin subtlety, tormented in his soul and his conscience, Pius XII knew the realities of man and of this world. Having at his disposal

Pius XII's Revision is just about as many informants on doings in Poland as there were Catholics in that country, he knew what stance to take regarding the real lot of both Catholics and Jews inhabiting a territory which, according to the various, breeds of Papées, was dotted throughout with gigantic "extermination camps", themselves equipped with extraordinary execution gas chambers.

Pius XII had his religious and political conception of good and evil but, all the same, did not believe, like an uncouth individual of the calibre of today's American president, in the political embodiment of good and evil. He believed, if one may put it thus, neither in Father Christmas nor in ogres and the idea of playing the part of universal Bogyman would not have occurred to him. His experience of political life and his knowledge of history allowed him to make a judgment of men, regimes and causes.

He felt an aversion both for National Socialist racialism and for the inhumanity of Soviet bolshevism. Whilst harbouring a great mistrust of Hitler (whom his collaborator Mgr Tardini dubbed "the motorised Attila") he felt the most acute fear in the face of Stalin, champion in the field of the closing or destruction of Christian places of worship, of the killing by firing, squad or deportation of priests and nuns, by mandatory atheism. On April 29, 1919, when nuncio in Munich, Pius XII had personally come quite close to being shot by a revolver-wielding Spartakist in a city fallen prey to the Reds and their exactions [26]. The Pope, let us repeat, had a weakness for France, felt affection for the Poles, admiration for the English, and a particular regard for the German people (but not for the Führer and his men) and he counted on a victory by the Americans whilst all the time dreading lest they allow the Communist Moloch to absorb a good part of Europe. In October 1939, when drafting his pontificate's inaugural encyclical (*Summi Pontificatus*), he inserted a passage on the sufferings and the future "resurrection" of the Polish people; the Allied aviation was to release 88,000 copies of his text over German territory [27]. In his boldness he would go so far, in 1939-1940, as to plot against Hitler in accepting to serve as a link between the British government and the German resistance; then, in early May 1940, he warned the Allies that a German offensive was imminent, providing important specifics. The Germans did not fail to learn of this and, in their view, his act of espionage put an end "to the neutrality of the Pope, apostle of peace". But it is to be noted that those same Germans nevertheless did not carry out any reprisals; besides, what could they have undertaken against such an impressive force as that of the Pope? [28] On May 10, 1940, the day of the German invasion of Holland, Luxembourg and Belgium, Pius XII sent similar telegrams to Queen Wilhelmina, Charlotte of Luxembourg and King Leopold III to express his compassion for them in the plight inflicted on their lands by Hitler's armies. Mussolini voiced strong discontent at the gesture. According to Italy's ambassador to the Vatican, Pius XII's reply was: "Let come what may! Let them even come and get me and take me away to a concentration camp! [29]" It is clear that the neutrality and impartiality of this sovereign pontiff are but a myth. Pius look sides with the Allies, a choice that did not stop him from voicing protets, through his representatives, against the atrocious nature of the anglo-American bombing raids.

BETWEEN HITLER AND STALIN, PIUS XII CHOSE STALIN

In 1941, after Germany's entry into war with the Soviet Union, most Catholics in the United States rejected the idea of economic and military support for Stalin. Did not the latter preach, with iron and fire, as far westward as Spain, a Communism that the papacy had declared to be "Intrinsically wrong"? In his 1937 encyclical *Divini Redemptoris*, Pius XI had slated: "Communism is intrinsically wrong, and no one who would save Christian civilisation may collaborate with it in any undertaking whatsoever" (*Communismus cum intrinsecus sit pravus, eidem nulla in re est adjutrix opera ab eo commodanda, cui sit propositum ab excidio chritianum civilemque cultum vindicare* [30]). With those words the Pope had condemned what was called at the time "the policy of extending the hand of friendship" to the Communists. But Roosevelt wanted to enter the war against Hitler. For him, all lies serving that purpose became permissible. On numerous occasions, and with insistence, he promised the Americans that their boys would never be engaged in a foreign war and, simultaneously, he prepared the economy of the country for war. He repeatedly committed the gravest provocations towards Germany and on August 14, 1941 issued with Churchill what is customarily called the "Atlantic Charter", whose sixth point called for nothing less than the "destruction of Nazi tyranny"! Roosevelt wanted to paralyse anti-war sentiment in his own country. To do so, he particularly needed to relieve the many millions of American Catholics of their scruples at the idea of having to help Stalin. Turning then to the Pope, he asked him, through the offices of American prelates discretely but duly coached on the matter, to intervene in that respect. Roosevelt, as will be noted yet again, shrank at no lie. Here we may quote Pierre Blet regarding a personal message from the US leader handed to the Pope on September 10, 1941:

> According to the president, religion was not completely outlawed in Russia, and there was hope that after the present war the Russian government would consent to religious liberty. "Insofar as I know", he added, "some churches are open in Russia" [31].

Actually, in huge Russia there were a total of two churches open - and closely observed by the police - , one in Moscow, the other in Leningrad. Overcoming his repugnance for Communism, slaughterer of priests in Russia, Spain and elsewhere, the Pope took it upon himself to convey the necessary instructions to the leading clergy in America; it was understood that the business would be carried out with the utmost discretion; the case to be put to the American flocks was as follows: *it is to the Russians and not to the Communist regime that the hand of friendship would be extended (and weapons supplied)* [32]. This argument of pure casuistry also served as a basis of the policy adopted by the doubtless reluctant Churchill and De Gaulle in favour of Stalin and the Communist parties at war with Hitler, Mussolini, Pétain.

In acting thus, Pius XII was lacking in effort to abide by the impartiality that, he said, he had always imposed on himself. The government of the Third Reich had solicited his approval of an "anti-Bolshevik crusade" which, the Germans held, when victorious, would enable the Russians, freed from the Soviet yoke, to regain the free exercise of their faith. The Vatican refused. A double standard was applied. It must be thought that, in this instance, to extend a hand of friendship to the Germans would have been to extend it to the National Socialist regime. *So it was that the German army was to see its soldiers, many of whom were Roman Catholics, and their chaplains get themselves killed in the East by American weapons supplied to the Communist regime with the Pope's secret blessing.* In Germany there was free exercise of the Catholic religion. Moreover, the Church was generously financed by the State; processions and pilgrimages mobilising thousands of the faithful were held freely, in the presence of the religious, civil and military authorities; churches were built, soldiers in uniform could attend services and take communion. All this apparently no longer counted in the eyes of Pius XII who, when approached and asked to do so by the Americans, had decided to choose Stalin against Hitler.

EFFECTIVE IN HIS WORK TO AID THE JEWS

Pius XII also took the liberty of infringing the laws in force and of breaking his word by having Jewish or non-Jewish members of the Resistance, amongst whom some makers of false documents, safely housed in monasteries, convents and even in places to which the German embassy in Italy had given letters of protection. Whether directly or through his intermediaries he gave room and board to thousands of Jews not only in the buildings of 150 religious institutions in various spots throughout Italy but also in the Lateran Palace, Castel Gandolfo and other places within Vatican City. The purity of intentions being but a myth, it can hardly be asserted that with a nature so sensitive and a spirit so astute as his, he acted out of sheer hostility towards National Socialism; he may well have feared the parliamentary democracies' blackmail, extraordinary violence and inhumanity; Churchill, Anthony Eden and the Americans made no mystery of their intention, should the need make itself felt, to "pulverise" (sic) the Italian cities, including the Eternal City (with the exception of the Vatican territory which, in the event, however, did receive some bombs!). Pius XII's personal action and that of his representatives in favour, for example, of the Jews of France, Holland, Slovakia, Romania and Hungary are established by so many initiatives, interventions, public statements and layouts of money that it is enough to refer to the ample bibliography devoted to him to get an idea of those efforts.

In 1996, G. Riegner in person was to do justice to the extraordinary activity deployed by the Pope and his representative in Hungary, Mgr Angelo Rotta, addressing themselves to the Regent Admiral Horthy in attempts to spare deportation to large numbers of Jews of Hungarian nationality or residence: "The Vatican did nothing without notifying us beforehand. It reported everything to us", exclaimed Riegner, an official of the World Jewish Congress, in a television documentary on the wartime Pope. In Budapest, the Vatican's representatives obtained from the Germans the right to deliver safe-conducts to 15,000 Jews. In their worried state, a great many Jews feigned conversion to Catholicism so as to be able to show a certificate of baptism. One particular church in the Hungarian capital was to put down in its parish register, still consultable today, a surprising number of such baptisms. The above-mentioned documentary, made for the BBC by the Jewish producer Jonathan Lewis, is entitled "The Silence of Pius XII". Since its release in 1996 it has been broadcast at least twice in France by the Franco-German cultural channel Arte; the most recent showing was on March 6, 2002 (French title: "Le Pape, les Juifs et les Nazis"; German title: "Die Pabst, die Juden und die Nazis" - translator's note).

HE HALTED THE GERMANS' DEPORTATION
OF THE JEWS OF ROME

That documentary, although hostile to Pius XII, features princess Enza Pignatelli-Aragona, who tells of the arrest and deportation, in October 1943, of a thousand Roman Jews (a move decided by German authorities alarmed at the proliferation in the city, before the approach of the Allies, of communist resistance members and other persons who might endanger security of their troops). This testimony puts paid to the myth according to which Pius XII witnessed, without raising an eyebrow, the arrest of the Jews of Rome "beneath his windows". The princess relates that she, when awakened at 4 a.m. by a telephone call from a Jewish friend, went straight to a neighbourhood near the Tiber where she could see that Jews were being put aboard some German lorries. She hurried to the Vatican palace, where, she had privileged access. She found the Pope at prayer in his private chapel and informed him of the hardship befalling "those poor people". Most upset| he immediately telephoned his secretary of State Mgr Maglione, who during the day made contact with the Reich's representative, Ernst von Weizsäcker. The latter, no more a Nazi than his predecessor Diego von Bergen, deftly intervened, talking with Berlin. With the agreement of general Rainer Stahel, head of the German garrison in Rome, he decided to put the case that these arrests, internments and transports placed too many constraints on the army. Other Germans also intervened, amongst whom the consul general, Albrecht von Kassel, and the rector of the German Catholic church in the city, bishop Alois Hudal. Berlin was to proceed with no further deportations of Jews with the exception of that of a convoy made up of Jews detained by the Italian authorities on individual grounds. Thus, in the circumstances in question the Pope demonstrated not indifference to the fate of the Jews but rather compassion and, better still, immediate effectiveness.

THE ALLIES' FIRST DECLARATION ON THE "GERMAN ATROCITIES" (DECEMBER 17, 1942): NO "GAS CHAMBERS"

On December 17, 1942, the Allies released a joint declaration on the "bestial policy of cold-blooded extermination" being carried out by the Germans against the Jews of Europe. Upon a rereading of the phrase today, one risks being led to believe that the Allies then had in mind "genocide" and "gas chambers". But to abide by that notion would be to commit an anachronism.

Examined closely, the text of the declaration reveals that the Allies had in mind: 1) the transporting of Jews in reputedly horrible and brutal conditions; 2) for the Jews who were in good physical form, slow death in forced labour camps; 3) for unfit Jews, abandonment in the cold and starving to death or being finished off in massacres; 4) a number of victims "reckoned in many hundreds of thousands". All of which is rather a long way from a *plan* of *mass murder of all the Jews* with, for most of them, *asphyxiation in chemical slaughterhouses immediately on arriving in camps designed far an extermination of industrial character*. Besides, at the time the declaration was taken for what it was: the denunciation (in a grandiloquent style required by the subject and circumstances) of crimes imputed to the enemy. The Germans, at their end, sometimes employed the same fighting rhetoric and, in some of the public speeches given by their lenders (Himmler, for one), readily promised the enemy's "extermination" (*Ausrottung*, in the broad sense, or *Vernichtung*). Furthermore, in all wars, including the one described in the *Iliad*, does not either side promise the other its ineluctable "extermination"?

This declaration was signed by the governments of the United States, Britain, the Soviet Union (unmatched specialist in deportations and camps!) and by nine others, amongst which, for France, the "National Committee" in London. It was read before the House of Commons by Eden, then Foreign Secretary, and in the Lords by Viscount Simon, Lord Chancellor [33].

Two days later, on December 19, the information bureau of the People's Commissariat for Foreign Affairs of the USSR issued the statement in a greatly modified version, enriched with remarks on Hitler's "cannibalistic plan" for the extermination of the Jews, and specifying:

> Besides machine-gunning men, women and children, people are murdered
> in specially equipped gas-chambers, electrocuted, burnt en masse. The
> inmates of concentration camps are poisoned with prussic acid [34].

This version was to be carried on the 21st by *Soviet War News* (n°443), a
Soviet publication printed in London. In that paper is found one of the first
mentions, in a document emanating from an official body, of the existence
of Nazi gas chambers (the rumour of "gassings", bearing no specifics, had
for its part begun circulating in the summer of 1941 [35]). Apparently no one
picked up and relayed this "intelligence" which, had it been lent credence,
should have made the front pages of the main Anglo-American newspapers.
Let us note in passing that this publication in the official Soviet press]
constitutes, along with other things, disproof of the Jewish contention
that] the Soviets passed "the martyrdom of the Jew" over in silence.

THE ALLIES' SECOND DECLARATION (AUGUST 29,1943) IN ITS DEFINITIVE VERSION: STILL NO "GAS CHAMBERS"

Eight months afterwards came the second Allied declaration on the crimes
imputed to Germany, which provides a particularly instructive case study
for the historian.

In its editions of August 30, 1943, the *New York Times* announced
that on the previous day, the United States and Britain had advised "the
Nazi killers" that they would punish them for their crimes in the occupied
countries and, particularly, in Poland ("US and Britain Warn Nazi Killers").
The article carried the two Allied powers' declaration in its entirety, and
dealt with the forced movements of populations in certain Polish provinces,
(The Jews were not mentioned.) It held that a number of victims were
killed on the spot and that males aged between 14 and 50 were being sent
to work in Germany. There followed a paragraph about children:

> Some children are killed on the spot, others are separated from their parents
> and either sent to Germany to be brought up as Germans or sold to German
> settlers or dispatched with the women and old men to concentration camps.

So far, nothing out of the very ordinary.

THE SAME DECLARATION
IN ITS ORIGINAL VERSION: "GAS CHAMBERS"!

On the other hand, for the historian of rumours this text is one of the most interesting in existence, particularly as concerns the history of the immense and obsessive rumour that founded the religion of the "Holocaust". It so happens that, in its initial form, the statement in question did indeed contain a formidable accusation against the "Nazis", that of having used homicidal gas chambers. The original draft, in effect, contained the passage:

> [...] dispatched with the women and old men to concentration camps where they are now being systematically put to death in *gas chambers* [my emphasis].

Why, one may ask, did this last clause of a sentence, still present in the Allies' paper on August 27, vanish and so fail to appear in the final declaration of the 29th, reproduced the next day in the press? The answer is as simple as can be: the British pointed out to the Americans that there was "insufficient evidence" thus to affirm the existence of homicidal gas chambers. The Americans concurred and decided to eliminate the last part of the sentence with its mention of the "gas chambers".

On August 24, the British had committed the rash act of sending the first draft to the Soviets, suggesting that they, at their end, release a similar declaration. Then, after some thought, they changed their position. They had realised that evidence was lacking "to justify the statement regarding execution in gas chambers" and, by virtue of the above-mentioned accord between themselves and the Americans, "it has been agreed to eliminate" the contentious fragment. Consequently, the Americans asked their ambassador in Moscow to notify the Soviet commissariat for Foreign Affairs "of the change in text".

As has been seen above, the Soviets, for their part, had spoken of gas chambers and even of killings by electricity eight months previously.

HOW THE ALLIES ABANDONED THE "GAS CHAMBERS"

What would have happened had the Anglo-Americans, deciding to maintain the original text, accused the Germans before the world of using homicidal gas chambers in their camps? Can one suppose that the accused would have leapt at the occasion of the slanderous charge to demonstrate, also before the world, that the Allied propaganda was shamelessly lying? In fact, the German authorities would most likely have treated that sort mad invention with contempt. Identical cases lead one to believe that the Germans would have reported the statement without even commenting on it, or else tagging on a merely ironic commentary. An attitude which, course, can only be deplored, for with the advantage of hindsight, one may unhappily note today that the hoax of the Nazi gas chambers, despite absurdity, was to enjoy incredibly good fortune.

On the first draft of the Anglo-American statement and on the decision - a revisionist one - to cut out the clause of a sentence that mentioned the "gas chambers", one may consult the text of the two telegrams that Cordell Hull, head of the State Department, sent from Washington to ambassador in Moscow; they are reproduced in *Foreign Relations of the United States. Diplomatic Papers, 1943*, (United States Printing Office Washington, 1963, vol. I, p. 416-417). The second and final draft, in which there no longer appears any mention of the "gas chambers", can be read in the aforementioned issue of the *New York Times*.

The same newspaper was to publish three months later a third official statement on the German "atrocities" [36]. Signed by Roosevelt, Churchill and Stalin, it contained no mention of either "gas chambers" or Jews; on the other hand, with a fine cynicism, the Germans were blamed for the "wholesale shooting of Polish officers"; this was a transparent allusion to the massacres of Polish prisoners of war in Katyn forest and elsewhere in Russia. However, today it is well known that those methodical killings were in reality perpetrated on the personal order of Stalin. Let it be said in passing that here is an example of how little credibility could rightly be accorded to the Allies' "intelligence" about German atrocities. If they were consistent in their logic, Pius XII's accusers, who rebuke the Pope for having kept quiet about the "extermination of the Jews" despite the "intelligence" he received from the Allies (in reality, from certain Jewish or Allied propaganda agencies and pressure groups), should also take him to task for not having denounced the "German" crime of Katyn and for thus having, by his silence, exonerated Hitler of a "Nazi horror" of which he had been duly "informed".

THE POPE'S FIRST DECLARATION (DECEMBER 24, 1942)

As if in echo to the Allies' first declaration of December 17, one week later, in his first radio message of Christmas Eve, 1942, the Pope decided to say a word about the deportations and the concentration camps of the Third Reich. The Jews were designated, although not mentioned as such but rather as persons being persecuted simply for belonging to a certain race. Likewise, Poles, or other people were designated, albeit not specifically, as being persecuted solely for their nationality. Unlike the Allies, the Holy Father also expressed his solicitude for all victims of all bombing raids. In a war, everyone suffers, the future victors along with the future vanquished and, in modern warfare, civilians die as well as the soldiers at the front. Stating his hope to see those who deplored the war and "aspire to the service of the human person and of his common life ennobled in God" vow not to rest until they had formed "a vast legion", the Pope cried out:

> Mankind owes that vow to the countless dead who lie buried on the field of battle. The sacrifice of their life in the fulfilment of their duty is a holocaust offered for a new and better social order.
>
> Mankind owes that vow to the innumerable sorrowing host of mothers, widows and orphans who have seen the light, the solace and the support of their lives wrenched from them.
>
> Mankind owes that vow to those numberless exiles whom the hurricane of war has torn from their native land and scattered in the land of the stranger, who can make their own the lament of the prophet: "Our inheritance is turned to aliens, our house to strangers" [*Hereditas nostra versa est ad alienos, domus nostra ad extraneos*, Jeremiah, *Lamentations*, 5.2]
>
> Mankind owes that vow to the hundreds of thousands of persons [*alle centinaia di migliaia di persone*] who, without any fault on their part, sometimes only because of their nationality or *race* [talora *solo per ragione di nazionalità o di* stirpe], have been consigned *to death or to a slow decline* [*sono destinate* alia morte o ad un progressive deperimento - my emphasis].
>
> Mankind owes that vow to the many thousands of non-combatants, women, children, sick and aged, from whom aerial warfare, whose horrors we have from the beginning frequently denounced, has, without

discrimination or through inadequate precautions, taken life, goods, health, home, charitable refuge or house of worship *.

Too often the Italian word *"deperimento"* is translated by "extinction", "annihilation" or even - outrageously - by "extermination". Let it be made clear here that the Pope never spoke of "slow *extermination*" but of "slow *decline*".

THE POPE'S REVISIONISTS WORD IN CONFIDENCE TO THE AMERICANS

There have at times been those who deplore the brevity of this evocation of the deported and interned Jews' lot; such people hardly bother to note that the Poles' circumstances were dealt with in just the same way. However this apparent timidity of the Pope, in reality his moderation, is explained by what must indeed be called a caution of revisionist character. At the Vatican, one Harold H. Tittmann was assistant to Myron Taylor, president! Roosevelt's personal representative. On December 30, 1942 he had a forty-* minute conversation with the Holy Father, who warned him anew that if the Allies bombed Rome, he would have to raise a solemn protest, and that would harm their cause, particularly in Latin American public opinion; Then the conversation turned to the Christmas radio message, the Pope saying that everyone, in his view, must have understood his allusion the Poles, the Jews and the hostages. On the subject of atrocities he had not been able to name the Nazis for then he would have had to name the Bolsheviks as well, which, he added, would not have pleased the Allies overmuch. Tittmann, in his account of the talk in a report addressed to the State Department and dispatched to Washington through the offices of the US envoy to Berne, wrote:

> He stated that he "feared" that there was foundation for the atrocity reports of the Allies but led me to believe that he felt that there had been some *exaggeration for purposes of propaganda* [my emphasis]. Taken as a whole he thought his message should be welcomed by the American people and I agreed with [him] [37].

British historian Owen Chadwick, who believes in the "genocide" of the

Jews and the "gas chambers", carries out a suggestive comparison between, on the one hand, this account of atrocities as such and, on the other hand, the way in which it was received first by the Allies, who minimised the data carried therein, then by the Pope who, careful to avoid exaggeration, diminished those data still further. Chadwick claims to note here a phenomenon that he deems regrettable and that, with Pius XII, might be explained by a sort of candour:

> Even in this utterance the Pope was very careful to guard against exaggeration. The story was, two million Jews killed for their race. The Allied Declaration [of December 17, 1942] had not believed it, and said *hundreds of thousands*. The Pope says, *some hundreds of thousands*. The story was that they were *all* killed *just* for their race and this was true. The Pope says they were *sometimes* killed only for their race, [in Italian] *talora*, on occasion. Like the minds of most of western Europe, the mind of the Pope was not bad enough to believe the truth. Like the high officials of the British Foreign Office he thought that *the Poles and the Jews exaggerated for the sake of helping the war effort* [38] [my emphasis].

Here the historian commits a slight error. The three numerical estimates given, respectively, first by "the news", then by the Allies and, finally, by the Pope were not 1) two million; 2) hundreds of thousands; 3) some hundreds of thousands, in that order, but rather 1) two million; 2) many hundreds of thousands; 3) *centinaia di migliaia* (hundreds of thousands). This decrease is, in effect, significant: the Allied authorities mistrusted the figures peddled by the (Jewish) agencies and groups and the papal authority, in turn, was wary of the figures trumpeted by the Allies. For the remainder, Chadwick is right: where the Allies presented all the Jews as being uniformly victims of a "policy of cold-blooded extermination" because of their race, the Pope said only that it was "at times" (*talora*) that such a state of things obtained. There never existed a German order, either textual or otherwise factual, to kill a Jew because he was a Jew and, on the contrary, examples are not lacking of Germans of the period, even in the midst of the war, even in Poland, Russia or Hungary, who were convicted by civilian or military courts for having killed just a single Jew or Jewess.

THE POPE'S SECOND DECLARATION (JUNE 2, 1943)

On June 2, 1943, in an address to the College of Cardinals, Pius XII stated:

> Moreover, you will not be surprised, venerable brethren and beloved
> sons, if our soul reacts with particular emotion and pressing concern to
> the prayers of those who turn to us with anxious eyes of pleading, in
> travail because of their nationality or their *race* [*travagliati come sono
> per ragione della loro nazionalità o della loro* stirpe] before greater
> catastrophes and ever more acute and serious sorrows, and destined at
> times, without any fault of their own, *to exterminating harassments* [*e
> destinati talora, anche senza propria colpa,* a costrizioni sterminatrici
> - my emphasis].

In its printed form, this passage appears in a section of the speech headed "Sufferings of peoples for reasons of nationality or race. The smaller nations". By "smaller nations" the Pope meant both the small States and the ethnic minorities of Europe. He evoked "these particular groups, subjected! to very harsh misfortunes" (*questi gruppi particolari, soggetti a più acerbis sfortune*). He recalled instances of relief of their sufferings obtained by the Holy See, the requests made on their behalf for a "sincere return to the elementary norms of law and humanity" (*ritorno sincere alle elementari norme del diritto e dell 'umanità*), even if at times the Vicar of Christ had found himself "before a door that no key could unlock" (*davanti a porte che nessuna chiave valeva ad aprire*).

IN 1943 AND 1944, THE POPE WAS TWICE A "REPEAT OFFENDER"

I am unaware if, amongst the great many authors who have devoted their efforts to the subject, there have been any to point out, and underscore, certain important facts: Pius XII was, in a way, a "repeat offender" in his daring to have those two documents *printed* not only in Latin in the *Acta Apostolicae Sedis*, the official record, but also in Italian. That of December 24, 1942, broadcast over Vatican Radio, was printed in 1943 in Rome proper, and not in Vatican City, by San Paolo editions in volume 4 of a collection entitled *Atti e discorsi di Pio XII*; the passage reproduced immediately above appears on pages 327-328. As for the address of June 2, 1943 to the College of Cardinals, it is in volume 5, issued in 1944; the parts reproduced or quoted above can be read on pages 134-135. I am not in a position to specify in what months of 1943 and 1944, respectively, those two volumes appeared. Mussolini was arrested, by order of the King, on July 25, 1943 and the Allies were to enter Rome on June 4, 1944; in the meantime, the real power in Italy passed to the German army and police. It must therefore be noted that the printing of the first volume, as well as that of the second (or, at the very least, the preparatory work for it), date from a period in which Fascists and National Socialists are said to have exercised an authority readily described as unlimited. If such were really the case, it would mean that Pius XII had taken the risk of defying that authority, thereby offering us one more example of his boldness. But, honestly, was there boldness in defying two powers,the Fascist and the National Socialist, that were being steadily deserted by the fortune of arms? It took more daring to stand up to the formidable power of the Allies and their capacity of retaliation by aerial bombardments than to confront Mussolini or Hitler who, besides, were not in the class of tyrants like Stalin, who enjoyed unbridled power. In these circumstances, the papacy, though without a single armoured division at its disposal, constituted all the same a force with which to be reckoned, and with regard to which Concessions were in order. It reigned over half a billion souls at a period When the world's population was two billion.

THE POWER OF THE PAPACY

People are wont to describe Adolf Hitler as a dictator of terrifying power, this point of view, Pius XII would appear to have been at the tyrant's mercy, to have lived in dread of bringing reprisals on himself, ever fearful least he arouse the Führer's wrath by intervening more on behalf of the Jews. For instance, in Holland, had the clergy not made a grave mistake in taking up the defence of the Jews? Had its intervention not had the effect of irritating the Germans? Had not the latter, on that occasion, proved their capacity of retaliation in deporting, by way of a special measure, a certain number of Jews who had converted to Catholicism, and, amongst those persons Edith Stein? Had Pius XII not at times confessed his inability to pronounce "fiery words" or to open a door "that no key could unlock"? For his part, had not Joachim von Ribbentrop, the Third Reich's Foreign

Minister, let it be understood that he had at his disposal means to put|
pressure on the Pope? I shall not deal here with the alleged plan to have
Pius XII abducted by the SS for, as O. Chadwick shows, that was a rumour
concocted and launched by the aforementioned British propaganda bureau
called "Psychological Warfare Executive" [39].

In reality Hitler was a good deal weaker and Pius XII much stronger
than is generally admitted nowadays. The Führer had scarcely any means
to intimidate Pius XII. Towards the end of 1942, von Ribbentrop ordered
Diego von Bergen, his ambassador in Rome, to threaten the Pope with
reprisals. The ambassador carried out the order. Pius XII responded at first
by silence, then, very calm, retorted that he cared not,what fate had in store
for him and that in the event of conflict between the Church and the State
it was the State that would lose [40]. Quite early on, a good part of the world
had ended up turning away from Hitler and joining the camp of the future
winners; after some time hardly anyone cared to maintain contact with the
pestiferous one; the neutral countries wound up adopting an attitude of
"active" neutrality in favour of the United States and Britain. Hitler had
to fight on land, on the seas and in the air against foes who had very much
the upper hand through their natural resources, armament and propaganda
(Goebbels had but mediocre resources on the international level). Under
siege in the illusory "fortress Europe", Hitler also had to defend against a
growing "terrorism" and a domestic "resistance" that undermined even the
state apparatus. A hunted man, he had no way out for, from January 1943
and their meeting at Casablanca, Roosevelt and Churchill were demanding
"unconditional surrender". Pius XII, on the contrary, was in demand and his
support or intervention was sought by all parties to the conflict. His standing
had become considerable in Europe, Central and South America, Canada,
the United States; the number of diplomatic representations to the Vatican
during the war and their activity bear witness to this fact, whereas before
the war, around 1936, that activity had been slack or nearly non-existent [41].
Even the British and Americans were present at the Vatican, alternatively
addressing to the "Pope-King" their tributes, promises and threats.

In Germany proper in 1933 Catholics numbered more than twenty
million, and with the Reich's recovery of the lands that had been torn from
it by virtue of the Versailles diktat they were to number rather more in the
following years; Chancellor Hitler would have been running the greatest of

risks in alienating so many of his compatriots of Roman Catholic obedience by striking a blow against the papacy.

The application of the Concordat, signed in July 1933, had, subsequently, greatly disappointed the two parties thereto, but Hitler could not defy its clauses too openly. He was conscious of the high clergy's deep hostility. Prelates like Faulhaber (labelled the *Judenkardinal* by certain National Socialists), von Preysing or von Galen showed a state of mind bordering on open rebellion, and Hitler could do nothing about it. According to some authorities, he kept on paying his Catholic's tithe to the treasury; according to others, he waited till 1943 to stop contributing. Numerous members of the German clergy got themselves noticed for their "resistance". Others had been publicly denounced for crimes against morals; in that era, Germany was the only country in the world no longer practising the fairly hypocritical custom of covering up, by agreement with the religious authorities, cases of paedophilia when clergymen were involved; it seems that the Vatican was rather loath to welcome this innovation by the Third Reich (where, it may be pointed out in passing, homosexuality between consenting adults was not, apart from some exceptions, against the law; homosexuality was essentially outlawed only as concerned the corruption of minors, equally prohibited in the parliamentary democracies; the Hitler regime interned such offenders in forced labour camps, where the pink triangle on their uniform distinguished them from other internees). All such churchmen, when found guilty or placed under suspicion, whether as "political offenders" or "common criminals", were arrested and, for the most part, gathered in the Dachau concentration camp where their living conditions, harsh as they might be, were envied by a good many other detainees.

A CLARIFICATION ON THE DUTCH JEWISH CONVERTS
TO CATHOLICISM

Pope Pius XII's defenders readily bring up the affair of the Dutch Jews who had converted to Catholicism. They like to say that, if the Pope had spoken out against the extermination of the Jews, then the Germans, by way of reprisals, would have further aggravated their victims' lot. They invoke the example of the Netherlands: in that country, the Catholic hierarchy had spoken out against the deportation of Jews still adhering to Judaism and, in reaction, the Germans carried out the reprisal of deporting Jews who had converted to Catholicism, Edith Stein amongst them. However, the comparison is invalid for the simple reason that the affair happened not at all as is generally related.

In the Netherlands, the high officials of the Catholic and Protestant churches had telegrammed a joint message to Reichskommisar Arthur Seyss-Inquart protesting against the Jews' deportation. Seyss-Inquart reassured them saying that converted Jews would not be deported; only those adhering to Judaism would be. At the same time, he expressly forbade them to read out the text of that enflamed protest to their congregations. But, on July 26, 1942 the religious leaders of all Christian denominations flouted that prohibition. Better still, the Catholic hierarchy, for its part supplemented the fiery message with a reading from the pulpit of a pastoral letter ending with a prayer whose words were a provocation towards the occupation forces:

> Thus, dear faithful, let us pray to God to accord forthwith, by the intercession of the Mother of Mercy, a just peace. To comfort the people of Israel so sorely afflicted in these days and bring them the true salvation in Christ Jesus. [...] Let us implore His aid for all who are afflicted and oppressed, for the prisoners and hostages, for the many who are under threat and in danger of death [42].

Seyss-Inquart, who had nothing of the fanatic about him, thus found himself obliged to carry out his threat. In its defence, the Catholic hierarchy piteously brought forth the argument that "the Reichskommisar's point of view had not been known in time everywhere". For more details on the matter, one may refer to my article of November 4, 1998 entitled "Six Questions to John-Paul II about Edith Stein" [43]. We may add finally that the Germans appear to have put their threats into effect only in a small proportion, and that many converted Jews were not, in reality, deported from Holland. According to the findings of an inquiry made by the aforementioned BBC television producer Jonathan Lewis [44], the number of arrests of such persons leading to their deportation was, all told, ninety-two [45].

The argument drawn from the case of the converted Jews is, consequently, of no great worth. As for certain utterances of Pius XII on his own impotence in some cases and for those of von Ribbentrop on his own means of coercion, they are to be judged in careful view of the circumstances in which they were made and of the persons to whom they were addressed. They remained mere Words.

THE CHURCHES' SHOW OF STRENGTH
ON THE OCCASION OF THE "FABRIKAKTION"

An example of the churches' strength against the National Socialist regime is supplied by the episode known as the *Fabrikaktion* (Factories operation) of February 27-28, 1943, in Berlin. At that period Germany was in the grip of the defeat at Stalingrad. Accordingly, three days of mourning had been decreed by Hitler. It was a tragic state of things. The authorities decided that it was no longer possible to let tens of thousands of Jews, some of them working in factories side by side with other Germans, stay in Berlin: The risks of sabotage were too great. Goebbels, in his capacity as chief of police of the capital, had thousands of Jews arrested. Of these, about 2,000 were interned in a group of buildings in Rosenstrasse and slated for deportation to the East. A number of them were married to Christian women. The latter, rising up in revolt, demonstrated outside the buildings in question for several days and nights, demanding the complete release and freeing of their husbands. Goebbels yielded; they won: Germany In her entirety would see no more attempts to deport Jews married to Christians [46]. The Vatican, for its part, seems not even to have had the time to intervene, the Christian reaction being so spontaneous and immediate. During the summer of 1943 Clemens August von Galen, bishop of Munster (Westphalia), attacked in his preaching the methods of the German police. Some National Socialists called for his execution. Goebbels was against the idea and "decided 'that the population of Munster could be regarded as lost [*for the National Socialists*] during the war, if anything were done against the Bishop... [plus] the whole of Westphalia' [47]". Furthermore, "as a whole, the measures considered by Eichmann's departments against Jews married to Catholics and against children of mixed marriages were not carried out in the Reich, either in Berlin or Vienna [48]".

If the Third Reich had wanted to exterminate the Jews, there can be no doubt that von Galen ("the Lion of Münster") and his like would have denounced from the pulpit such a criminal undertaking that, what with its gigantic dimensions, could not have been going on unnoticed.

THE ACCUSATION ALLEGEDLY BROUGHT AGAINST THE VATICAN BY SS OFFICER KURT GERSTEIN (APRIL-MAY 1945)

Kurt Gerstein (1905-1945), a mining engineer with a degree in chemistry as well, joined the National Socialist party in 1933 and enrolled in the SA. In 1936 he was excluded from the party for anti-State activities. He was interned twice for some weeks in 1936 and 1938. A Protestant, he was an active member of the Confessional Church, opposed to the regime. Rehabilitated, he entered the SS in 1941. Appointed to the SS Institute of Hygiene in Berlin with the rank of sub-lieutenant (special assignment), he was in charge of disinfection and the fight against epidemics. Few details are known of his life in the period between June 1942 and March 1945. It is recorded that in April 1943 he was promoted to lieutenant (special assignment) and that he was twice hospitalised, first in March 1944 in Helsinki, then in Berlin in the autumn of that year; the reasons for this double hospitalisation are unknown. In late March 1945 he left the capital of the Reich to rejoin his wife and children in Tübigen. On April 22 he turned himself in to the French 1st Army. Placed under arrest and taken to Paris, he was questioned by officers of the *Organe de recherche des crimes de guerre* (ORCG). Detained at the Cherche-Midi prison, he was charged with murder and complicity in murder. On July 25, 1945 he was found hanged in his cell.

Two months before his death, the prisoner had given his various interrogators or jailers a series of confessions, each more stupefying than the rest: two versions are dated April 26, a third bears the date of May 4 and three others May 6. In them Gerstein claimed to have been witness in August 1942 to gassings of Jews at Belzec (and, secondarily, at Treblinka). Describing the Belzec gassings, he stated that the killers used the emission fumes from a Diesel engine (an engineer and chemist all in one ought to know that such gas is one of the very least appropriate for killing!). The victims, as many as 700 or 800 at a time, had been packed, standing, into the gas chamber; it was an enclosure measuring 25 square metres and 45 cubic metres, which leaves one to suppose that from 28 to 32 persons had stood in a space of one square metre, under a 1.8 metre ceiling (once again, where is the engineer?). At Belzec and Treblinka the Germans, according to him, had killed 20 million Jews (in another version, 25 million); however, the Jewish authors affirm for us that from 1939 to 1945 Jewish deaths in all the camps and ghettos, in the towns and in the countryside, in all the acts of reprisal, on all the battlefields, in all the bombing raids, all the evacuation marches, all the deportation convoys amounted to a total of six million. A pile of shoes taken from victims measured, according to Gerstein, 25 metres in height (another version: 35-40 metres) (here as well, engineer Gerstein engineer did not specify how shoes were thus projected or placed up to the level of a 10- to 12-storey building). Gerstein "confessed" that at Auschwitz, a camp to which he had never been, several million children were killed by having a wad soaked in hydrogen cyanide placed under their noses! Again according to his testimony, one day general Globocnik assured him that, two days previously, Hitler and Himmler had themselves been at Belzec; however, neither Hitler nor Himmler ever visited that part of Poland.

It would take far too long to list all the absurdities, implausibilities, inanities and contradictions contained in the six versions of this confession, along with their "supplements", addenda and rough drafts. Thus the holocaustic authors who claim to reproduce these texts have made a good number of amputations, alterations and fabrications in their attempts to dissemble the truly zany character of it all. Léon Poliakov has been the most dishonest amongst them. For the trouble that he brought on himself In 1981 with his manipulations and fabrications of texts attributed to Gerstein I refer the reader to the entry under his name in the index of my *Écrits révisionnistes (1974-1998)* and, in particular, to pages 568-572 therein. In 1961, in the first edition of his work of reference (*The Destruction of the European Jews*), Raul Hilberg, the veritable Pope of exterminationism, mentioned Gerstein's name twenty-three times. But, in early 1985, during the first trial of Ernst Zündel in Toronto, Hilberg, appearing as witness and expert advisor to the prosecution, was to undergo the ordeal of a cross-examination concerning his use of the extravagant testimony in question. He ended up denying practically any value to Gerstein's confessions; on this score as well one may consult my *Écrits révisionnistes* for the verbatim transcript of the concessions that the greatest specialist of the history of the so-called "Holocaust", when cornered, had to make (p. 956-957; www.ihr.org/books/kulaszka/09hilberg.html). Confronted with such or such passage of the confession, Hilberg found himself obliged to speak of "pure nonsense", of a "totally false statement", "sheer exaggeration", a "far-out statement". At his end, Pierre Vidal-Naquet, who in 1979, along with L. Poliakov, had not shrunk at invoking Gerstein's testimony as proof of the existence of the Nazi gas chambers [49], saw himself compelled a few years later to admit that "the six versions of the testimony... are crammed implausibilities and contradictions [50]". But, as early as in 1968, another specialist, Olga Wormser-Migot, had expressed her own scepticism. She wrote of "a confession of which a fair number of parts remain obscure" and concluded: "For our part, it is difficult to acknowledge the full authenticity of Kurt Gerstein's confession - or the veracity of all its elements [51]".

Never in his "confession" does Gerstein claim to have had any contact with Pope Pius XII or even with his representative in Berlin, the nuncio Cesare Orsenigo. He simply states that he once presented himself at the nunciature door to reveal his secret and was asked to leave because he was a soldier. It is true that he adds a claim to have made a verbal report to Dr Winter, the bishop of Berlin's secretary, as well as to quite a number of other persons, Protestants or Catholics: to a Swede, to a Swiss, to members of the Dutch resistance, to factory workers, to "thousands" of people, he asserts. He never speaks of a written report. Moreover, after the war, no trace was ever found of any report addressed by Gerstein either to the nunciature or to the archbishop of Berlin, and nothing either at the Vatican or in the Swedish, Swiss, or Dutch archives. Those who, shortly after the war, asserted that Gerstein had spoken to them of the horrors in question made no written report of it either for themselves or for their superiors Such was the case, in particular, of the Swede von Otter.

Hence, the accusation that the Protestant Kurt Gerstein is supposed to have brought against the Vatican is reduced to practically nothing. For all the trouble taken, why should his confession not be used to attack the Protestant churches just as well, since he also claims to have informed Otto Dibelius and Martin Niemöller's family? Why not use the same weapon against Sweden, Switzerland or the Netherlands which, if he is to be believed, Gerstein also notified orally of the atrocities?

The first author to open everyone's eyes to the flimsiness of Gerstein's testimony was Paul Rassinier. He did so in his 1961 book *Ulysse trahi par les siens* (La Librairie française, Paris), and never quit going over the the matter in other writings, up to his death in 1967. In the same revisionist line, after my own publications and after the humiliation inflicted on Raul

Hiberg on the subject in early 1985, one may refer to two scholarly works: Carlo Mallogno's *Il rapporto Gerstein: Anatomia di un falso. Il campodi "sterminio" di Belzec*, (Sentinella d'ltalia, Monfalcone - Italy, 1985), and Henri Roques's thesis, presented at the University of Nantes on June 15th of the same year and published the following year by André Chelain in his *Faut-il fusiller Henri Roques?* (Should Henri Roques be shot?), (Polémiques, Paris, July 1986) [52]. Just recently, the same Henri Roques made an astounding discovery concerning the decidedly troubled personality of K. Gerstein [53].

One may dispense with reading *Kurt Gerstein ou l'ambigüité du bien* (Castermann, Paris, 1967, with an afterword by Léon Poliakov) by Saul Friedlander, who is not afraid of falsifying the documents that he reproduces. On the other hand, the same author's *Pie XII et le IIIe Reich Documents* (Seuil, Paris, 1964) is worth a look, but only for Alfred Grosser's interesting afterword.

THE ACCUSATION BRAZENLY BROUGHT AGAINST THE VATICAN BY THE PROTESTANT ROLF HOCHHUTH (1963)

Born in 1931, German author Rolf Hochhuth completed in the spring of 1962 a stage play entitled *Der Stellvertreter.* The hero is an imaginary figure, the young Jesuit father Riccardo Fontana who, deeply distressed by what another character, Kurt Gerstein, discloses to Pius XII about the Nazi gas chambers, realises that the Pope is not going to denounce the horror. A humble prelate, he dons the Jewish star and accompanies a convoy of Jews in a gas chamber to meet his death. According to the interpretations, the play's name (in English, *The Deputy* in its American editions, *The Representative* in its British ones) designates either the young Jesuit, in which case it would be fitting to translate the German title into French as "Le Remplaçant" ("The Replacement") or "Le Substitut" ("The Substitute"), or else it means the Pope directly and is to be rendered by "Le Vicaire" since, as is well known, the Pope is the "Vicar of Christ". In French the title *Le Vicaire* has been established by usage.

This ponderous Germanic tragedy, written in free verse in the plodding style of the expressionists, takes place over five particularly indigestible acts and brings together no fewer than forty actors. The author is keen to advise us beforehand: "Aside from the Pope, the Nuncio, Gerstein, [professor] Hirt and Eichmann, all characters and names are fictitious But one may rightly say that those five historical characters are, themselves as well, transformed into imaginary creations. Hochhuth demonstrates the clumsiest fantasy in his dealing with history. The sixty-five pages of explanation ("Sidelights on History", "Epilogue") that he thought it a good idea to add on to the printed version of his play amount to no more than a compilation of more or less historical dates reported in the tone off novelist or newspaper hack. In short, it is all a load of the worst so-called "historical" novel style or of Piscator drama, and yet it is this dubious creation, launched at the time like a new grocery brand, that the media of the whole world have succeeded in presenting as one of the most serious indictments of Pius XII.

As regards the text of the play in its English version one may consult Rolf Hochhuth, *The Deputy*, (Grove Press, New York 1964), with a foreword by Albert Schweitzer; the "Sidelights on History" and the "Epilogue" from page 287 to page 352. Paul Rassinier, he again, took the whole business apart in *L'Opération "Vicaire". Le Rôle de Pie XII devant l'Histoire*, (La Table Ronde Paris 1965) [54].

ACCUSATION RESUMED WITH CHUTZPAH IN AMEN, A JEWISH FILM (2002)

Early in 2002, a big media racket was made for the launching of the Jewish film *Amen*, produced by Claude Berri, written by Jean-Claude Grumberg, directed by Constantin Costa-Gavras, with Mathieu Kassovitz in the lead role and incidental music by Amar. Tedious and lie-ridden, this 2-hour, 10-minute film takes its inspiration from the figments of Hochhuth's lively imagination and from *Shoah*, Claude Lanzmann's fictional work. Clichés follow one another thick and fast, with the incessant to-and-froing of the deportation trains, full on leaving and empty on returning, with loutish German soldiers revelling in the spectacle, observed through a spy hole, of the death of Jews in a gas chamber, with the banquet at the Vatican where guests feast on scampi (of course!) whilst the Jews are dying, with Eichmann waltzing at a ball or in a spirited exchange of ribaldry amongst friends, with gigantic pyres for burning the Jews (in front of which German soldiers move about untroubled by the heat, like diabolical creatures having no need of protection, being in their element) and with the young Jesuit who, naturally, is going to show off his Jewish star in front of Pius XII. The film swarms with novelistic inventions, one of the more mendacious consisting in showing Gerstein and the Jesuit listening to Vatican Radio on Christmas Eve 1942, both in the hope that the Pontiff will, in his talk, speak out against the horrors being visited on the Jews; an authentic recording of the broadcast is distinctly audible, but Costa-Gavras brazenly skips over the passage on the *"progressivo deperimento"* endured by the persecuted Jews. This cut from the text of the Papal message is deliberate and allows Costa-Gavras and his accomplices to have their audience believe that Pius XII said nothing of the Jews' hardships. The subterfuge also enables them to depict the consternation of the two listeners to the radio, Kurt Gerstein and Riccardo Fontana, and to Underscore the Pope's cruel indifference, if not his fundamental cowardice.

Thus the historian need not dwell on this 100% kosher production in which effrontery vies with judeocentricity. On the occasion of the film's release an article that was rather well informed about the realities of the story and Costa-Gavras's falsifications of it appeared in the French weekly *Valeurs actuelles* [55].

PIUS XII CASTIGATED FOR HIS RESISTANCE AND REVISIONISM

Pius XII, to the end, resisted the pressure of certain Jewish organisations. He refused to endorse either the nascent religion Of the "Holocaust" (an imposture) or the creation of the State of Israel (another imposture, directly linked to the first). He was to pay a high price for his daring, if but posthumously.

Who can stand firm under the pressure and in the face of powerful Jewish organisations and their campaigns? Practically no one. These institutions' hold on the media, their perpetual moaning and recriminations, their systematic recourse to blackmail, their practice of telling lies designed to throw others way off track, the fear that they inspire (*metus Judaeorum*), their frenzy (be it real or make-believe), and their contempt for those who do not belong to the chosen people end up sweeping aside all obstacles. In order, suddenly, for such organisations not to be strictly obeyed it takes some exceptional historical circumstances. Then the humiliated, maligned, duped or colonised goyim take the risk of holding up their heads and sometimes, go so far as to rebel against their tyrants. The hoax or religion of the "Holocaust" has progressively built itself up since beginning with rabbinical lies born in Central Europe; thereafter, with the aid of propaganda, those inventions were exported to Western Europe (including the neutral countries, the Vatican and bodies like the International Red Cross). Once in place they spread throughout the United States, where they benefited from the staging provided by Hollywood and the rest the media. They came back with all the more force from 1945 onwards to pour into the heart of Europe. They strongly contributed to the creation of the State of Israel, a source of conflicts to come. They poisoned the post war world. The ferment of hatred that an imposture of these dimensions leaves in people's minds, still infects our society nowadays. Prodigious financial extortions, grounded in intimidation or blackmail, have for half a century been feeding the trade, the business, the industry of the Shoah. One would almost say that the heads of these Jewish groups had done their best to strengthen, for the anti-semites' satisfaction, all the stereotypes of the Jew as a liar, a crook, alternately whining and arrogant, crying out for vengeance till the end of time and everywhere demanding his pound flesh. These Jews have resurrected Shylock [56].

Unable - and for good reason - to prove the reality of the alleged "destruction of the European Jews" or the alleged "Nazi gas chambers" the Jewish pseudo-historians or scientists à la Raul Hilberg have ended up, capitulating. They have passed the baton to the novelists à la Elie Wiesel, the playwrights à la Hochhuth, the film directors à la Lanzmann or Costa-Gavras, to the illustrators, poster-makers, painters, creators of monumental "sculptures" and designers of exhibitions in "Holocaust" museums of every, sort, to the musicians, advertisers, sponsors of ceremonies, demonstration organisers, tour operators for school trips to Auschwitz. What remains today of veritable historical research into the lot of the Jews of Europe during the last war is heavily tainted by the cult of Jewish "remembrance".

The offensive launched against Pius XII, especially since the 1960s, bears the stamp of this general transformation running from an abortive historical and scientific inquiry to the "criminal" indictment by theatre, cinema and all the performing arts that address the imagination. In the first stages, there were attempts, like Saul Friedlander's in 1964, to draw up the brief on Pius XII in line with the historical record, which was, after all, a normal thing to do. That brief was all too obviously composed solely of material from the accusation and it proved to be so meagre that, little little by little accusers had to abandon the realm of history and science for that of fiction. It was in this spirit that the same Friedlander, in his forementioned 1967 book, and Pierre (Weil) Joffroy, in 1969, set their hearts on some madcap writings of an SS officer immortalised for the circumstances as "God's spy", and becoming, in a way, Saint Gerstein (cf. The latter author's *L'Espion de Dieu. La Passion de Kurt Gerstein*, Grasset, Paris; English edition: *A spy for God: the ordeal of Kurt Gerstein*, Collins, London, 1971). From this fiction was made, in Hochhuth's The Deputy, a play where imagination was given still freer rein. Forty years later, even though Saint Gerstein's confession is discredited and Hochhuth's phantasmagoria forgotten, a Costa-Gavras and his acolytes have returned to the rubbish bins of history to pull out *The Deputy* and recycle it in the form of a delirious film that they gracefully entitle *Amen*. To have it plainly understood that Pius XII said "amen" to National Socialism and gave it his blessing, they top off the job with a poster where the Christian cross and the swastika unite, a work of art owed to the talent of the Jew Oliviero Toscani, former staffer of the knitwear merchants Benetton. All told, a fake Pius XII has been fabricated just as a fake "Holocaust" was fabricated. And, in both cases, where the historian's work had failed, the resources of the imagination, so dear to fraudsters, were summoned.

PIUS XII'S FIRST SUCCESSORS YIELDED TO THE JEWS WHILST AT THE SAME TIME RESISTING

Pius XII's first successors gave in to the Jewish pressure, albeit without going so far as final surrender. John XXIII (deceased in 1963) conceded much to the lobby but he did not utter the awaited words on the alleged extermination and the alleged gas chambers. He is said to have written a "Prayer for the Jews" in which, addressing himself to God, he evokes "the beauty [sic] of Thy Chosen People"; he asks that the Christians be forgiven for having treated the Jews as Cain had treated his brother Abel and for thus having, a second time, crucified the son of God in the flesh of the Jews. But this "prayer" is a mere fake, launched, in English, by the American Jewish Committee's monthly *Commentary* a year and a half after John XXIII's death [57]. In France, the daily *Le Monde*, with full knowledge of the facts, ended up contributing, in its turn, to the diffusion of this Jewish sham. [58]

The "prayer" still passes for genuine with too many Roman Catholics today, even though the Vatican has pointed out its apocryphal character.

Until his death in 1978, Paul VI followed a line of conduct identical to that of John XXIII. During the war he had been deputy secretary of State at the Vatican: "In that capacity, [he] had a conversation in 1945 with Gerhart Riegner, during which he doubted Riegner's word that 1.5 million Jewish children had perished in the Holocaust [59]". On January 5, 1964, on the occasion of his visit to Jerusalem, he avoided the "pilgrimage" to the "Holocaust" memorial of Yad Vashem, sending a member of his delegation instead.

John Paul I, who served as Pope for only thirty-three days, had not enough time to face the Jews' anger and demands. But the machine was up and running: sooner or later, what with their way of playing, notably with the success of that "prayer of John XXIII", the programme would be carried out as announced and the Vatican would bow. That is what came to pass with John Paul II.

JOHN PAUL II RESISTED FOR ELEVEN YEARS, THEN CAPITULATED

Acceding to the papal throne in 1978, John Paul II started out resisting Jewish pressure, then, in his turn, yielded on a good number of points, particularly in the affair of the Auschwitz Carmelite nuns. Towards the end of his eleventh year, precisely in the course of that issue, he ended up capitulating. On August 26, 1989, in a message to Polish bishops, he wrote of "the massive extermination of the Jews, who were doomed to the gas chambers". Then, on September 26, 1990, he declared to a group of Poles at a Vatican audience:

[The Jewish] people lived side by side with us for generations, on the same land, which became, as it were, a new fatherland of their diaspora. This people underwent the terrible death of millions of their sons and daughters. At first they were stigmatised in a particular way. Later, they were pushed into the ghetto in separate neighbourhoods. Then they were taken to *the gas-chambers,* and put to death - *simply because they were children of this people* [60] [my emphasis].

Thus, in his person, the Vatican, forty-four years after the end of the Second World War, came to endorse the story, albeit fictitious, of the "Holocaust" with its gas chambers and its millions of Jews (if not its "six million") killed because they were Jews.

Two years later, on November 7, 1992, *L'Osservatore Romano* condemned historical revisionism for casting doubt on the "Holocaust". It stated: "There is no historical revisionism that can call into question the inhuman abyss of the Holocaust" (*Non c'è revisionismo storico che possa rimettere in discussione I'abisso disumano dell'Olocausto*).

In 1993, the Vatican, after refusing to do so for forty-five years, recognised the State of Israel.

In 1998, on the occasion of the canonisation of Edith Stein, John Paul II again affirmed the existence of the Nazi gas chambers:

> Because she was Jewish, Edith Stein was taken with her sister Rosa and many other Catholic Jews from the Netherlands to the concentration camp in Auschwitz, where she died with them in the gas chambers. Today we remember them all with deep respect. - From now on, as we celebrate the memory of this new saint from year to year, we must also remember *the Shoah, that cruel plan to exterminate a people - a plan to which millions of our Jewish brothers and sisters fell victim* [61] [my emphasis].

March 12, 2000 the same Pope, at a ceremony in Saint Peter's Basilica "penitential" liturgy had been created from scratch just for the event, solemnly expressed the Church's contrition for past wrongdoings and, in particular, for the sins committed against the Jewish people by numerous Christians. But, curiously, he failed to pronounce the word "Shoah". Immediately, Israel Landau, chief Ashkenazi rabbi of the State of Israel, stated that, although glad to hear the request for forgiveness, he was "deeply disappointed that the subject of the Shoah had not been dealt with". At his end, Jean Kahn, president of the Consistoire Israélite de France, rejoiced at the act of penitence but added: "We should have preferred that the Christian anti-semitism that led to the Shoah not be put on the same plane with the regrets concerning the Crusades, the Inquisition, the discrimination against women and the poor [62]". John Paul II was to effect his total submission in visiting, from March 23rd to 26th 2000, first Jerusalem, then Yad Vashem;

he made his penitents gesture anew and demanded "silence" on the Shoah. The word "silence" is obviously no longer to be taken in its normal sense of "muteness", like that for which Pius XII is rebuked, but in its Jewish denotation, inaugurated by Elie Wiesel, of "respectful impotence to relate the unspeakable suffering of the Jews". Already a few days before, bubbling over with admiration, Henri Tincq of *Le Monde* had written: "With regard to the Jewish people, [John Paul II] will have made steps that seemed unimaginable only thirty years ago [63]". A week later the Parisian journalist relapsed: "There is still room for work but, thirty years on [from the Vatican Council], progress is so rapid that it leaves the extremists of both sides giddy [64]". On March 26 John Paul II slipped a message into the Wailing Wall begging forgiveness: extracted from between the stones, his note was put on exhibit at Yad Vashem. In an editorial, *Le Monde*, never at a loss to carry on in Jewish-style one-upmanship, expressed its satisfaction but, as might be expected, deemed that it was not enough:

> It must be hoped that the Vatican will follow though to the end in its task and suspend, for instance, the process of beatification of Pius XII, and throw full light on its role during the war [65].

Here the newspaper was picking up a demand previously conveyed by Aharon Lopez, Israel's ambassador to the Holy See who, in 1998, had asked that the procedure in question be "frozen for fifty years" [66].

"WITH THE JEWS, IT'S ALWAYS *MORE*"

The Pope thus went "from the Shoah to *Techouvah* [in Hebrew: repentance]". To venture now to think that the Jews will consider themselves satisfied would be not to know them well at all. It must be said that, in line with the phrase of their friend François Mitterrand, "with the Jews, it's always *more*" (I take this item from a very close confidant of the late French president). Not only are they demanding that the process of Pius XII's beatification be suspended, but they are also voicing the same demand in regard to Pius IX (Pope from 1846 to 1878). The latter had made the young Edgardo Levi-Mortara his own adopted son to prevent him from being returned to his Jewish parents after a secret baptism. The ensuing affair gave rise to one of those international scandals that the Jewish communities periodically set about orchestrating. The Jews even mobilised on their behalf such figures as French Emperor Napoleon III and Franz Josef of Austria. But Pius IX held firm: a stubbornness for which, a hundred and thirty years later, the Jews are today preparing to make him pay [67].

THE *ACTES ET DOCUMENTS DU SAINT-SIÈGE RELATIFS À SECONDS GUERRE MONDIALE*

Yet another insistent demand: that for an opening of the Vatican archives. From 1965 to 1981, a team of four Jesuits appointed in 1964 by Paul VI had, at the request of Jews who were demanding clarifications on the subject, published the eleven tomes (in twelve volumes) of the *Actes et documents du Saint-Siège relatifs a la Seconde Guerre mondiale* (*ADSS*). But in these twelve volumes, the result of considerable effort undertaken in the face of their pressure, the Jews did not find what they had hoped to see, that is, material with which to prove Pius XII guilty. Subsequently, they came charging back demanding to be able to enjoy a privilege unexampled in the history of the Roman Catholic Church: that of having access personally, although not being even members of the Church, to the Vatican archives (which were not yet classified and catalogued!). Put another way, they set forth the following line of reasoning to John Paul II: "Your four Jesuits may perhaps have cheated in presenting these documents; we want to go into the archives and see for ourselves; if you refuse us permission to do so, you'll be giving us reason to believe that Pierre Blet, Robert Graham, Angelo Martini and Burckhart Schneider have effectively cheated". In October 1999, the Pope bowed and created a mixed commission made up of six historians - three for the Christians, three for the Jews - assisted by four rapporteurs, in order to examine, indeed make an appraisal, of the twelve volumes' contents. The three Catholic academics were the Americans Eva Fleischner, Gerald Fogarty and John Morley; the three Jews were militants of the anti-revisionist cause: Michael Marrus (from Toronto), Bernard Sucheky (from Brussels) and Robert Wistrich (from Jerusalem).

In May 2001, the French historian François Bédarida, since deceased, published an article in the review *Esprit* entitled: "Pour faire avancer l'histoire: les archives du Vatican 1939-1945" (p. 15-25). This Catholic of Jewish origin, animated by a Judeo-Christian hatred of revisionists, expressed his wish to see "openings of the Vatican archives [to 'researchers'] to be made, doubtless in a gradual and measured manner" (p. 25). He thus made himself the spokesman of his Jewish colleagues in the mixed commission who, for their part, were demanding an unlimited opening of the not yet catalogued Vatican archives. Such an exigency is materially impossible to satisfy; no one in charge of a collection of archives in the process of being organised (which is the case at the Vatican for all the period from 1922 onwards) can halt a monumental project to devote himself suddenly to a job that would mobilise all his material, financial and human resources? and imperil the continuation of his normal work. Nonetheless, thanks to the Vatican's positive attitude, a solution was found and accepted by both sides: the members of the commission were to be able to get all the clarifications they desired on any given point. They need only submit their queries to father Peter Gumpel who, with his team, would have to do the necessary research work and provide answers.

On July 20, 2001 there was a dramatic turn of events: the mixed commission announced to the Vatican hierarchy that it was suspending its work. On the 23rd, the World Jewish Congress had the nerve to declare that the decision was taken after the Vatican's refusal to open its archives to the historians. For once, the Vatican was to show a loss of patience and protest vigorously. On August 7, father Gumpel, assigned by the Pope with the task of speaking about the dossier, said that "certain Jewish historians of the commission" were to blame for this failure through their "improper" and "irresponsible" conduct. He called into question the seriousness of some Jewish members who seemed not even to have read the twelve volumes that they were supposed to be studying. In October 2000, the group had formulated forty-seven queries with a view to clarifying various points. P. Gumpel had taken the trouble to prepare, in reply, forty-seven files. However, according to him, due to "transverse" dissensions (we may gather that here it was no doubt a matter of disagreements between, on the one hand the commission's Catholic members and, on the other hand, the Jewish ones) it had been possible to examine only twelve of the questions. And he went on to add: "It is a lie to say that we haven't been willing to provide answers; I was at their disposal [68]". In a press release of August 25, father Gumpel's accusatory remarks received a rather unexpected corroboration, coming as it did from Cardinal Walter Kasper, the Vatican official in charge of relations with Judaism. Shortly before, the Cardinal of Baltimore, Archbishop William Keeler, had provided details, including the names of those involved, regarding the unacceptable behaviour of his compatriot, the Jew Robert Wistrich, member of the mixed commission, and of Seymour Reich, president of the International Jewish Committee for Interreligious Consultations (IJCIC), a regular partner in the dialogue with the Vatican. In particular, "leaks" had been organised by these Jews with the intent to fuel a campaign against the memory of Pius XII [69]. In preparing those "leaks", the Jews in question had failed to honour their commitments to discretion and thus swindled those who had put their trust in them. Shamelessly publishing the fruits of their larceny, they coupled the information with a lie-ridden commentary of their own making. They knew that the Vatican could not make a rebuttal precisely because of the commitments to discretion made on either side. In short, by so cheating they had won the match. Doubtless they became aware of the quality of the dossier established by the four Jesuits, who had done so much work in producing the twelve-volume *ADSS*. Sensing that they were once again heading towards failure in their campaign to denigrate Pius XII's image, it is likely they had sought to cause a diversion in organising the "leaks", which allowed them to get out of a tight corner. They obliged the Vatican to take responsibility for a possibly definitive break.

In 2002 French author Gerard Leclerc produced a work bearing the title *Le Bricolage religieux* ("The religious do-it-yourself", Éditions du Rocher, Paris). That same year he also wrote an article judiciously headed "Le Mythe des archives du Vatican" [70]. He showed that Jewish historian Annette Wieviorka was not in the least entitled to denounce any "stubborn closure" of the Vatican archives, or to believe that "the Gerstein report" might be found therein. He recalled that Pierre Blet had never found a trace of such a report. He specified that it was for "technical" reasons that authorisation to re-examine the archives was withheld. He added that John Paul II had nonetheless decided to bring forth the dates by which results were expected "in announcing that, as of 2003, six hundred and forty files concerning relations between the Holy See and Germany under Pius XI would be available, and that shortly afterwards the same would go for the pontificate of Pius XII". He concluded: "Perhaps things will go the same way with the Vatican archives as with the treasures of the Knights Templar. But serious historians will have to swear off clinging to the myth".

ASSESSMENT

The Jewish authorities, so quick to demand of the goyim in general and of the Church in particular acts of penance and reparations of all kinds, would be well advised to take stock of themselves with regard to their own actions in the past. Zionism and National Socialism, so similar in their respective ideologies, collaborated solidly before and during the Second World War [71]. If the "Nazis" committed crimes against the Jews and others, the Zionists and the "Brown Jews" had their part in such doings. Where, in this case, is the penitence of the leading rabbis? Furthermore, the Jews played a decisive role in the birth and development of Communism, an ideology which, in concrete terms, has inspired and justified some especially murderous undertakings. Also in this respect, no words of penance have been heard from the worldwide Jewish community. To advance the claim that the Jews were the first people to suffer from Communism is to show a real brass neck. When, for instance, the sons and daughters of Israel had managed to occupy in strength and in numbers the highest spheres of the State, as was once the case in the Soviet Union, and when the moment of the inevitable purges came, it only remained to them to purge one another, which, for that matter, they did in only a relative measure since, in the last analysis, millions of Jews alleged to have been at first exterminated by the Germans, then, it is added, decimated by Stalinism, have survived very well indeed up to our day in Russia, the Ukraine, Israel and other places.

With the accusation and defence briefs fully prepared, the case of Pius XII is a clear one. The accusation's file is empty whereas that of the defence abounds in evidence and documents establishing that the Pope did not render himself guilty of any "silence" on the true sufferings of the Jews during the war. The relentlessness of so many Jewish organisations against a Pope who did so much on behalf of the Jews is particularly unjust, but in it one encounters a constant trait of these bodies: they bite even the hand that feeds them. They have a habit of demanding everything; then, when their demands have been met, they openly insist on obtaining still more. Unable to get "more than everything", they grumble, remonstrate, then fly into a rage. There are two sorts of historical revisionism that these Jewish organisations do not tolerate: the revisionism of those who are hostile or indifferent to the Jews and the revisionism of those who are sympathetic to them. And the latter annoys them more than the former. It proves, in effect, that even some of the minds most favourably disposed towards them refuse to believe in the Great Lie [72].

CONCLUSION

How is it that the "trial of Pius XII" is still going on in our day?

The blame lies partly with the defence, whose Counsel have played the accusation's game. Without demanding to see any proof thereof, they have from the very start admitted the argument of the alleged "Holocaust", a sort of *a priori* that the accusers impose as a historically established truth. In doing so, Pius XII's defenders have gagged themselves. Henceforth they have only been able to make heard a few murmurs of protest. That is no way to present one's case. If the accused's barrister adopts a line of defence determined by the public prosecutor, then it only remains for the judge and jury to pronounce a verdict of guilty: at the very best their judgment will take into account some mitigating circumstances.

Thus does Pius XII, "the Pope-King", join the vast cohort of victims, famous and obscure, who, since 1945, have been convicted by a thousand courts (beginning with the allegedly international (in reality inter Allied) military tribunal at Nuremberg) where the defence is in the hands of lawyers who, as in the witchcraft trials of yore, either cannot or do not know how to call into question a formidable taboo, or else do not wish to expose the accused or themselves to the risk that putting such an argument would entail; the taboo here, of course, is that of the purported "Holocaust" or "Shoah".

No lawyer has stood up to proclaim: "The abominable crime did not take place. And because it didn't take place, Pius XII cannot have been, either directly Or indirectly, an accomplice to that crime."

In the eyes of his accusers, Pius XII's crime was accompanied by an aggravating circumstance: a revisionist during the war, the Pope remained a revisionist after the war, up to his death in 1958. A revisionist can hardly be beatified, much less canonised, that is, placed amongst the saints.

As for Pope John Paul II, we have seen that he ended up, in 1989, sacrificing to the religion of the "Holocaust" and, in 1992, hurling his anathema at historical revisionism. But can one really hold it against him? The author of these lines should well be aware of what it can cost to face up to "an unbearable Jewish thought police" (as the late Annie Kriegel called it), and understands if no one desires in the least to incur the hatred and wrath of the Jews (*odium iramque Judaeoruni*), He knows, for example, that in trials where the judges' conduct is dictated to them by the "Holocaust" taboo, it is best to keep a low profile, as the expression goes. A Pope is vested with heavy responsibilities towards his flock. He is not going to jeopardise the entire Roman Catholic Church by adopting behaviour which, as justified as it may be on the moral plane, will set off a political and media earthquake of global dimensions.

But the historians who claim to defend the memory of Pius XII need not be preoccupied with such contingencies. They need only care about being exact. Paul Rassinier has shown them the way. In the review of the Pius XII case they ought, like Rassinier, to abandon the defence of connivance in favour of one that makes a break with the past. They would then be showing that the charge brought against the wartime Pope does not rest on any facts but only on a historical imposture, that of the alleged "Holocaust" of the Jews.

The task is easy in itself, but anyone who produces results through it will risk coming under the guillotine blade of special laws that in too many countries, and notably in France, hinder the researcher's freedom.

<h2 style="text-align:center">RECOMMENDED READING</h2>

Amongst the studies mentioned above, those to be kept in mind are, first and foremost, the twelve volumes of the *Actes et documents du Saint-Siège relatifs à la Seconde Guerre mondiale* (*ADSS*) (1965-1982) - of which only the first volume has thus far appeared in English as *Records and documents of the Holy See relating to the Second World War* (1968) - and the clear summary thereof published by Pierre Blet, SJ, *Pius XII and the Second World War: according to the Archives of the Vatican* (1999). In his *Britain and the Vatican during the Second World War* (1986), Owen Chadwick has penned a remarkably limpid work of scholarship in a delectable English (not to be missed is, by way of example, his portrait, on pages 13-14 and 310-317, of the British ambassador to the Holy See, Francis D'Arcy Godolphin Osborne who, in 1963, became Duke of Leeds).

Amongst the revisionist studies, the pages that the American Arthur R. Butz devotes to the Vatican's role during the war in his book *The Hoax of the Twentieth Century. The Case against the Presumed Extermination of the Jews* are a fitting complement to Paul Rassinier's *L'Opération*

"Vicaire" Le rôle de Pie XII devant I'Histoire (1965); they appear in to the work that professor Butz first published in England of which numerous editions have been produced since then United States by the Institute of Historical Review (PO box 2739, Beach, California 92659). At the time when Butz was preparing that appendix only nine volumes of the *ADSS* had been issued. In that piece he demonstrates remarkable qualities of analysis and synthesis, and his views are so penetrating that the subsequent publication of the last three left the accuracy of his diagnosis entirely intact. The attention given to the contents of the papers concerned makes these pages stand out as an anthology for the precise analysis of historical texts and documents. One may also read the same author's "Robert Graham and Revisionism" (*Journal of Historical Review*, vol. 17, n° 2, March-April 1998, p. 24-25) especially, "Pope Pius XII and the Jews" (*JHR*, vol. 17, n° 4, July-1998, p. 20-21).

Under the title *Une encyclique singulière sous le III Reich* (Vrij Historisch Onderzoek, Antwerp, 1999) the Belgian revisionist Pierre Maximin has published a particular study of the encyclical *Mit brennender Sorge* ("With a burning concern") devoted, in 1937, by Pope Pius XI to Socialist ideology (not named as such but designated). It is known that Eugenic Pacelli, the future Pius XII, contributed greatly to the drafting of the text. One may express reservations on the analysis proposed by P. Maximin. On the other hand, he is right in criticising the Pope for his silence or near-silence on the many crimes perpetrated against the vanquished. On June 2, 1945 Pius XII gave a speech before the College of Cardinals, the text of which Maximin had the good idea to include in his book (p. 121-123). This battle charge by Pius XII, blowing the trumpet of victory against a crushed enemy, is unworthy of a great Pope. At certain points, the tone resembles more that of a vengeful phillipic than a solemn address (*litterae solemniores*). The Pope is seen lashing out steadily at the "satanic spectre raised by National Socialism", at the inflictor of "persecution" and his "insolence". He accuses Hitler of been solely responsible for the new World War! He attacks him for concentration camps (in particular, Dachau) and for tortures carried with "the most exquisite scientific methods" as if the Allies, at, their end had not, at the very instant of his talk, their own concentration camps and their own torturers. At the end, the Pope attacked the defeated leader for having increased "the ranks of revolution and disorder, in the pay of a tyranny no less despotic than those for whose overthrow men planned*". Thus he imputed to Hitler, in good part, the success of Stalinist Communism! He did so at the very time when the Allies were able to gauge the dimensions of Bolshevism's conquests, which had only become possible thanks to Roosevelt, Churchill, de Gaulle and numerous other democrats, and with the blessings of a Pope who, as has been seen above, when he had had to choose between Hitler and Stalin, chose Stalin. At the moment when Pius XII was launching this enflamed anathema against a dead man, millions of European Catholics were beginning, with the Allies' assent, to live through horrors in comparison to which the hardships they had experienced due to Hitler would appear minor indeed.

Harold Tittmann III is the son of the "chargé d'affaires" who, during the war, was assistant to Myron Taylor, Roosevelt's personal envoy to the Holy See. In 2004, he published a book about his father: *Inside the Vatican of Pius XII, The Memoir of an American Diplomat During World War II* (Doubleday, New York, xii-224 p.). One may see, in particular, chapter two for a detailed account of the machination thanks to which, through their agreement, Roosevelt and Pius XII got around those American Catholics who were against both intervention in the war and Stalin. With the help of Pius XII, Roosevelt was, from November 7, 1941, able to bestow on his friend Stalin the benefits of the Lend-Lease Act, that is, weapons and money in abundance, all supplied by the American taxpayer.

Amongst the essays of Catholic or traditionalist inspiration in support of the wartime Pope one may note the Belgian author Alexis Curvers's *Pie XII, le pape outragé* (first edition by Robert Laffont, Paris 1964; second edition, revised and enlarged, by Dominique Martin Morin, Bouère, 1988). As for Mary Ball Martinez, Amercian journalist accredited at the Vatican from 1973 to 1988, she has made a summary of one aspect of her book, *The Undermining of the Roman Catholic Church*, and had it published in a piece entitled "Pope Pius XII During the Second World War" (*JHR* vol. 13, n° 5, September-October 1993, p. 26-29). The "poignant" letter said by her to have been addressed by Pius XII to Myron Taylor seems apocryphal. In this purported letter, of which she provides neither the date nor the source, the Pope expresses his regret at having kept silent, during the conflict, about the Russian Communist regime at President Roosevelt's behest.

Retired French general Jacques Le Groignec, for his part, upholds the classic argument of Pius XII's defenders: "No one knew" (in French, "Personne ne savait", title of his article in *L'Action française*, March 22-April 3, 2002, p. 14). This line of reasoning, according to which even a Churchill was ignorant of what is commonly called "the genocide of the Jews", is, as has been seen above, both untenable (since the senior Allied leaders and the Pope could not lend credence to rumours which, after request for verification or inquiry, had proved groundless) and quite implausible (for if a slaughter of such gigantic proportions and industrial character had actually taken place, then the resulting death of six million Jews would not have escaped the general attention any more than would the disappearance of the entire population of a country like Switzerland).

In his *Sionismo e Fondamentalismo* (Controcorrente, Naples 2000), Curzio Nitoglia has reproduced in Italian Pius X's encyclicals on Fascism (June 29,1931), National Socialism (March 14,1937) and, finally, Bolshevik and atheistic Communism (March 19, 1937). These texts may also be read in official English translation at www.vatican.va/holy_father/pius_xi/encyclicals.

Again on the Internet, one may consult Paul Airiau's April 2002 article "Pie XII, le révélateur. Réflexions autour d'une controverse" (www.religioscope.com).

At times it happens that, by dint of so strongly wanting to defend the memory of a maligned Pope, some people end up echoing unfounded rumours. The French journalist Alain Barluet has recently reported that at Yad Vashem, in the "Valley of the Righteous", there is a tree planted in grateful tribute to Pius XII. That is an error. The same writer commits another error on the subject of the affair known as the "fifty kilos of gold". Home in September 1943 the Germans, in reprisal for the planting of a bomb outside one of their barracks, had demanded that quantity of gold of the City's Jews. Only thirty-five kilos were collected; therefore the Jewish community turned to Pius XII. The latter was quick to take the necessary steps to have the fifteen kilos that were lacking delivered but, suddenly, it became apparent that, thanks to the generosity of sympathetic Romans, the complement had already been found. Barluet is right to report that significant episode, but he makes a double error in taking up and putting his name to the legend that has it that the Pope effectively gave the Jews fifteen kilos of gold, and that, in order to enable him to do so, "the sacred chalices of the Roman parish churches had been melted down [73]".

NOTE: To go about claiming that Pius XII was "Hitler's Pope" one must be altogether ignorant of the friendship (there is no other word for it) that linked him to Franklin Roosevelt and led him to support the Rooseveltian policy of helping Stalin. On the subject of this friendship the reader may consult the *Wartime Correspondence between President Roosevelt and Pope Pius XII*, with an introduction and notes by Myron C. Taylor, Personal Representative of the President of the United States of America to His Holiness Pope Pius XII, The MacMillan Company, New York 1947, XVI-127 p. Roosevelt concluded his first letter (December 23, 1939) with these words: "To You, whom I have the privilege of calling a good friend and an old friend, I send my respectful greetings at this Christmas Season. Cordially yours, Franklin Delano Roosevelt" (p. 19).

Pius XII replied (January 7, 1940): "Recalling with keen joy the pleasant memories left Us after Our unforgettable visit to your great nation, and living over again the sincere pleasure that personal acquaintance with Your Excellency brought Us, We express in turn Our hearty good wishes, with a most fervent prayer for the prosperity of Your Excellency and of all the people of the United States" (p. 23). On February 14, 1940, Roosevelt spoke of "my old and good friend" (p. 31). On November 9, 1944, the Pope telegrammed Roosevelt to express his "heartfelt congratulations" on the American president's third re-election, achieved two days previously (p. 117).

Meanwhile, on August 30,1943, departing from his duty of impartiality, Pius XII complained to Roosevelt, in veiled terms, of the Germans, who were "shackling" the Italian people with their "formidable forces" and preventing them from enjoying peace (p. 99). On August3,1944, Roosevelt paid tribute to Pius XII for his action and efforts in favour of the Jews, instructing Myron Taylor to convey his praise with the following note: "I should like you to take the occasion to express to His Holiness my deeply-felt appreciation of the frequent action which the Holy See has taken on its own initiative in its generous and merciful efforts to render assistance to the victims of racial and religious persecutions" (p. 113). All by itself, that message renders laughable the subsequent attempts to portray Pope Pius XII as Hitler's Pope.

A NOTE ON YAD VASHEM AND ITS EUNUCHS

In 1963 Yad Vashem, the Israeli Institute for remembrance of the Shoah, created a "department of the righteous". This is a propaganda enterprise meant to illustrate the idea that, whilst hundreds of millions of goyim, from 1939 to 1945, proved either hostile or indifferent to the Jews, a handful of "righteous ones" did their duty.

As early as 1966 a tree was planted there in tribute to father Marie Benoît. As of December 2000, the number of righteous ones entitled to a tree or, for want of a tree, an inscription, was 2020.

The Comité français pour Yad Vashem, with offices in Paris's prestigious Avenue Marceau and whose honorary presidents are Samuel Pisar, Simone Veil and Ellie Wiesel, describes itself as an "association for the remembrance and teaching of the Shoah and for the nomination of 'Righteous ones among the Nations'." The words "Yad" and "Shem" (linked by the conjunction "Va") are borrowed from a fragment of Isiah's prophecy: "[For the Lord says:] And to them I will give in my house and within my walls a memorial...an everlasting name [a 'yad vashem'], that shall not be cut off [74]" The pronoun "their" designates the faithful eunuchs that will "keep the [Lord's] Sabbaths, choose the things that please [Him] and take hold of [His] covenant". The Lord promises: "Their burnt offerings and sacrifices shall be accepted upon mine altar" (King James Bible).

Notes

1. See Robert Fauisson, *Écrits révisionnistes (1974-1998)*, R. Faurisson, Vichy, 1999, p. 1844, 1889-1892 (vol. IV).

2. Eugemo ZOLLI, *Before the Dawn, Autobiographical Reflections*, Sheed and Ward, New York, 1954; for example, p 82-83; this book was republished in 1997, with the title *Why I Became a Catholic;* it has also been published in French translation (*Avant l'aube, autobiographie*, François-Xavier de Guilbert), Paris, 2001). One may refer as well to Judith CABAUD's *Eugenio Zolli ou le Prophèted d'un monde nouveau*, Francois-Xavier de Gambert, Paris, 2000.

3. Consultable at the Internet page www.catholicleague.org/pius/dalin.htm.

4. Walter LAQUEUR, *The Terrible Secret*, Weidenfeld & Nicolson, London, 1980, p.83

5. F.H. HINSLEY, *British Intelligence in the Second World War: Its influence on Strategy and Operations*, Vol. 2, HMSO, London, 1981, p. 673.

6. [Mark WEBER] "British Wartime Propaganda Lies", *The Journal of Historical Review*, vol. 18, nos. 5-6, September-December 1999, p. 15.

7. W. LAQUEUR, *op. cit.*, p. 63.

8. *Ibid.*, back cover presentation featuring a facsimile of the telegram.

9. *Ibid.*, p.237

10. *The Catholic Church and the Holocaust* 1930-1960, Indiana University Press, Bloomington, Indiana, 2000, p. 112.

11. Pierre BLET, S.J., *Pius XII and the Second World War: according to the Archives of the Vatican*, Paulist Press, New York, 1999, p.165.

12. *Nuremberg ou la Terre promise*, Les Sept Couleurs, Paris, 1948, p. 156-160

13. *Ibid.*, p 158. This work by M. Bardèche is classified *"Non communicable"* at the Bibliothèque de documentation Internationale contemporaine (BDIC) Nanterre university campus, just outside Paris.

14. *Ibid.*, p. 159-160.

15. James J MARTIN *The Man Who Invented "Genocide". The Public Career and Consequences of Raphael Lemkin*, Institute for Historical Review, Torrance, California, 1984, p. 39.

16. The very Catholic François Mauriac lent credence to this clanger of a tale on May 4, 1945 and reproduced it in 1950 in his *Journal*, IV, Flammarion, Paris, p.54.

17. Jean-Pierre LANGELLIER, "Les 'jumeaux-cobayes' d'Auschwitz témoignen, à Jérusalem", *Le Monde*, February 10-11, 1985, p. 4.

18. *La Montagne*, February 5, 1985, p. 8.
19. Paul EMMANUEL telling of his encounter with Simon Wiesenthal, the Nazi hunter, *Ciné-Revue* (Belgium), October 18, 1984.
20. *Trial of the Major War Criminals before the International Military Tribunal, Nuremberg, 14 November 1945-lst October 1946*, Nuremberg, vol. XVI, p. 528-529.
21. "Clio, dialogue de l'histoire et de 1'âme païenne" (July 1913), (*Euvres*, III, Gallimard, Paris, Bibliothèque de la Pléiade, p. 1187-1188.
22. M. PHAYER, *op. cit.*, p. 23; the source for this quotation is given in a note (n° 27) as "Report by the Polish Ambassador to the Holy See on the situation in German-Occupied Poland. Memorandum No. 79, May 29, 1942, Myron Taylor Papers, NARA [US National Archives and Records Administration]".
23. *L'Histoire*, March 2000, p. 40.
24. P. BLET, *op. cit.*, p. 141.
25. *Ibid*, p. 145.
26. Robert SERROU, *Pie XII, le pape-roi*, Perrin, Paris, 1992, p. 53.
27. Pierre BLET, *op. cit.*, p. 69-70; Marc-André CHARGUÉRAUD, *Les Papes, Hitler et la Shoah, Labor et Fides*, Geneva, 2002, p. 149. The official translation of this encyclical may be read at http://www.vatican.va/holy_father/pius_xi/encyclicals/documents/hf_p-xi_enc_19031937_divini-redemptoris_en.html.
28. Pierre BLET, *op. cit.*, p. 32-34, as well as M.-A. CHARGUÉRAUD, *op. cit.*, particularly in the section headed "Conjuration et espionnage", p. 85-87.
29. Dino ALFIERI, *Due dittatori di fronte*, Rizzoli, Milan, 1948, p. 22.
30. *Acta Apostolicae Sedis*, vol. XXIX, 1937, p. 96.
31. Pierre BLET, *op. cit.*, p. 122.
32. *Ibid.*, p. 116-122; M.-A. CHARGUÉRAUD, *op. cit.*, p. 95-99, for the section entitled "La faucille, le marteau et la croix du chrétien?" (The sickle, the hammer and the cross of the Christian?).
33. Hansard, *Parliamentary Debates*, December 17, 1942: House of Commons, cols. 2982-2983, and House of Lords, cols. 607-608.
34. Release on "The execution by Hitlerite authorities of the plan to exterminate the Jewish population in the occupied territory of Europe", reproduced in *Soviet Government Statements on Nazi Atrocities*, Hutchinson & Co., London, New York etc., 1946, p. 57-58.
35. James J. MARTIN, *The Man Who Invented "Genocide"*, *op. cit.*, p. 38-39.
36. "Statement on Atrocities", *New York Times*, November 2, 1943, p. 14.
• Extract from the full translation of Pius XII's talk presented in the *New York Times* of December 25, 1942, p. 10 - translator's note.

37. *Foreign Relations of the United States.* Diplomatic Papers, vol. II, Europe, Government Printing Office, Washington, 1964, p. 911-912.
38. O. Chadwick, *op. cit.*, p. 218.
39. Ibid., p. 275.
40. *Ibid.*, p. 218, with supporting references.
41. *Ibid.*,p. 1-6.
42. Christian FELDMANN, *Edith Stein, juive, athée, moniale,* Éditions Saint-Augustin (Switzerland), 1998, p. 138.
43. Robert FAURISSON, *Écrits révisionnistes 1974-1998, op. cit.*, p. 1880-1888; English translation below in Appendix III, p. 83.
44. See above, p. 30.
45. J. CORNWELL, *op. cit.*, p. 362.
46. *Encyclopaedia Judaica,* article "Berlin", p. 650; P. BLET, *op. cit.*, p. 154.
47. Franklin LITTLE & Hubert LOCKE (editors), *The German Church Struggle and the Holocaust,* Wayne University Press, Detroit, 1974, p. 121-122, quoted by M.-A. CHARGUÉRAUD, *op. cit.*, p. 74.
48. P. BLET, *op. cit.*, p. 154.
49. "Une déclaration d'historiens [contre R. Faurisson]", *Le Monde,* February 21,1979, p. 23.
50. *Les Assassins de la mémoire,* La Découverte, Paris 1987, p. 154; here quoted the English translation: *Assassins of Memory,* New York, Columbia University Press, 1992, consultable at www.anti-rev.org/textes/VidalNaquet 92b.
51. *Le Système concentrationnaire nazi* (1933-1945), Presses universitaires de France, Paris, 1968, p. 11, 424.
52. Reissued in 1989 by the same publisher under the title: *La Thèse de Nantes, et l'Affaire Roques.*
53. "Lettre à Henri Amouroux" of March 18, 2002, published in the *Bulletin d'information de l'Association Verité et Justice* (Switzerland), n° 15, April 2002, p. 3-4. See English translation below, Appendix IV, p. 95.
54. Republished in 2002 by La Vieille Taupe, Paris.
55. Laurent DANDRIEU, "Huit mensonges sur Pie XII", March 8, 2002, p. 70-71.
56. Edoardo LONGO, *Il Coltello di Shylock,* La Rocca d'Europa, Trieste, 2002.
57. F.E. CARTUS (pseudonym), "Vatican II and the Jews", January 1965, p. l9-29; the "prayer" appears on page 21.

58. R. FAURISSON, "Un Faux: 'La prière de Jean XXIII pour les juifs'", *Revue d'histoire révisionniste*, n° 3, November-December 1990-January 1991, p. 20-32; see English translation in Appendix I below, p. 71.

59. M. PHAYER, *op. cit.*, p. 211; source: John T. Powlikowski, "The Vatican and the Holocaust: Unresolved Issues" in *Jewish-Christian Encounters over the Centuries*, Marvin Perry and F. M. Schweitzer (editors), Peter Lang, New York, 1994, p. 301.

60. *L'Osservatore Romano*, 21 September 1990, p.l. (The English translation of the passage appears as quoted by a January 1991 "Pastoral Letter of the Catholic Bishops in Poland" consultable at www.jcrelations.net/en/?id=1037 - Translator's note)

61. *L'Osservatore Romano*, 12-13 October 1998, p. 6-7; entire speech consultable in English translation at www.vatican.va/holy_father/john_paul_ii/homilies/1998/documents/hf_jpii_hom_11101998_stein_en.html

62. H. TINCQ, "Réactions mitigées en Israël et chez les juifs de France", *Le Monde*, March 14, 2000, p. 40.

63. "De Cracovie à Jérusalem, le long parcours de Jean Paul II", *Le Monde*, March 18, 2000, p. 20.

64. "Jean Paul II à Yad Vashem, logique d'un itinéraire", *Le Monde*, March 25, 2000, p. 19.

65. "La force de Jean Paul II", *Le Monde*, March 28, 2000, p. 15.

66. *L'Express*, February 21, 2002, p. 12.

67. H. TINCQ, "Le souvenir d'un enfant juif trouble la béatification de Pie IX" (The remembrance of a Jewish child poses difficulties for Pius IX's beatification), *Le Monde*, August 25, 2000, p. 1.

68. Laurent MORINO, Rome correspondent, " Échec de la commission mixte sur la Shoah. Le Vatican 'charge' les historiens juifs" (Failure of the mixed commission on the Shoah. The Vatican "charges" the Jewish historians), *Ouest-France*, August 8, 2001, p.2.

69. H. TINCQ, "L'échec de la commission d'historiens chargée d'examiner le rôle de L'Église pendant la Shoah tourne à la polémique judéo-catholique" (The failure of the commission of historians in charge of examining the Church's role during the Shoah is becoming a Judeo-Catholic quarrel), *Le Monde*, September, 2001, p. 4.

70. *Le Figaro*, March 5,2002, p. 5.

71. Emmanuel RATIER, *Les Guerriers d'Israël*, Facta, Paris, 1995, and Jean-Claude VALLA, *Le Pacte germano-sioniste* (7 *août 1933*), Éditions de la Librairie nationale, Paris, 2001 (Les Cahiers libres d'histoire, n° 4).

72. In France, for example, the more favours the senior political leaders accord to the Jews, the less they are paid in return. Successive presidents have particularly coddled the Jews, but all, at the end of their term, have been the object of the vilest attacks on the part of Jewish organisations. Illustrations of this "law" have arisen with Charles de Gaulle, Georges Pompidou, Valéry Giscard d'Estaing and François Mitterrand. Hopeful of drawing a profitable conclusion from the unfortunate experiences of his predecessors, Jacques Chirac sought to break the spell by effecting straight away a total submission; first, he swore an oath of allegiance to the B'nai B.rith concerning his party's electoral policy, then, barely two months after becoming president, on July 16, 1995, at the "place des Martyrs Juifs du Vélodrome d'Hiver" in Paris, he pronounced the French Republic itself guilty of what the French State, under the German occupation, had done to the Jews. There then followed an avalanche of monetary and other compensations to the sole benefit of the Jews; finally, he personally condemned "revisionist arguments". He went so far in his obedience and toadying that, at the time of the 2002 elections, a Jewish journalist like Alain Mine could say that it was right to vote for Chirac to "reward" him (sic) for his statement of July 1995 (*Le Figaro*, May 2, 2002, p. 14). But sooner or later the leaders of the Jewish organisations will bite the hand that has fed them, for it remains ever in their vital interest to be able to declare themselves dissatisfied: anti-semitism is their money-maker and protesting their raison d'être.

73. "Dans la vallée des Justes", *Le Figaro*, February 26, 2002, p. 12.

74. Isaiah 56.5; the King James version reads: "Even unto them will I give in mine house and within my walls a place and a name better than of sons and of daughters: I will give them an everlasting name, that shall not be cut off." The "New Living Translation" (Tyndale House Publishers, Wheaton, Illinois, 1996) reads: "I will give them - in my house, within my walls - a memorial and a name far greater than the honour they would have received by having sons and daughters. For the name I give them is an everlasting one. It will never disappear!" André Chouraqui in his *L'Univers de la Bible* (Lidis, Paris, 1983) presents the passage as follows: "I give them in my house, within my ramparts,/ my hand and the name, better than that of sons and daughters./ I give them an enduring name that shall not be cut off." He explains that "house" designates the sanctuary of Jerusalem and that the coupling "the house and the name" is a Hebraism for "commemorative stone bearing an inscription". In regard to these eunuchs, dear to the Eternal One in both the Old and New Testaments, the *Book of Wisdom* ("Wisdom of Solomon") and the *Gospel according to Saint Mathew* (19.12) may also be consulted.

APPENDIX I

A FAKE:
"JOHN XXIII'S PRAYER FOR THE JEWS"

[November 1990]

"We are conscious today that many many centuries of blindness have cloaked our eyes so that we can no longer either see the beauty of Thy Chosen People nor recognize in their faces the features of our privileged brethren. We realise that the mark of Cain stands upon our foreheads. Across the centuries our brother Abel has lain in the blood which we drew or shed the tears we caused by forgetting Thy Love. Forgive us for the curse we falsely attached to their name as Jews. Forgive us for crucifying Thee a second time in their flesh. For we knew not what we did..."

This "prayer for the Jews" attributed to Pope John XXIII, who died on June 3, 1963, is a fake. This fake appeared in January 1965 in a "report" of the American Jewish magazine *Commentary* entitled "Vatican II and the Jews" under the by-line "F. E. Cartus" which, the reader was told, "is the pseudonym of a Roman Catholic observer who has watched developments at the Ecumenical Council very closely [1]".

The text's contents alone ought to have led the reader to think that a Pope, even one who was so very favourable to the Jews as Angelo Roncalli (1881-1963), could hardly express himself in such terms with regard to Catholics. The "prayer" amounts, in effect, to saying: the Jews are beautiful; they are God's chosen people; on their faces they bear the traits of our privileged brothers. For centuries, the Jews have shed blood and tears. We Catholics have been blind to all this. Our own faces are hideous in that they bear the mark of Cain. We are responsible for the blood and the tears shed by Jews. We have forgotten the love of God. We have lied in inventing the account telling that God cursed the Jews. It is we - and not the Jews who have crucified God. We were men unaware.

This text is excessive: it exudes too much hatred for some and too love for others.

In following the destiny of this "prayer" chronologically in the press, in France alone, from 1966 to the present day, one may notice that the fake was at first very quickly denounced, and that then, in the face of the repeated assaults by certain persons in favour of a text that was so interesting for the Jewish cause, the truth began to be silenced; soon the public was led to believe that it was an authentic document. The daily *Le Monde*, for instance, would try for a few years to put its readers on their guard against the fake, which it cautiously presented as "apocryphal", then abandoned any effort at clarification and even, as will be seen below, ended up giving the fake its implicit endorsement.

1966

In October 1966, under the heading "Une prière de Jean XXIII pour les juifs", *La Documentation catholique* published a text presented as the reprint of an article from *La Liberté* of Friburg (Switzerland) of September 9, which began thus:

> Vatican circles confirmed on September 7 the existence and authenticity of a prayer drafted by John XIII only a few days before his death in which he asks forgiveness of God for all the hardships that the Church has caused the Jews.
>
> The existence of this prayer which, according to its author's intentions, was to have been recited in all churches, had been announced recently during a lecture given in Chicago by Mgr John S. Quinn, who was one of the Council experts [2].

There followed the text of the "prayer". No precision was supplied as to "the Vatican circles" that had, reportedly, confirmed the item's authenticity, nor as to the source enabling the writer to state that, in line with the late Pope's intention, the "prayer" was to have been read out in all churches.

A month later, *La Documentation catholique* published a disclaimer entitled "La prière de Jean XXIII pour les juifs est un faux" (The prayer of John XXIII for the Jews is a fake). Here is the full text of that disclaimer:

> The office of the Secretary of State [of the Vatican] issued, on October 26, the following release concerning the so-called prayer of John XXIII published in our edition of October 2, col. 1728, in which we echoed

certain press information, adding no comments of our own:

"*La Documentation catholique* (October 2, 1966, n° 1479, col. 1728) reproduced, after *La Liberté* of Friburg of September 9, a 'prayer of John XXIII for the Jews' and stated that Vatican circles had confirmed its authenticity.

"It is, in reality, a fake.

"*La Liberté* of Friburg took the text in question from the Dutch newspaper *De Tijd* of March 18, 1965. *De Tijd* had got it from *American Commentary* of Chicago (organ of the American Jewish Committee) of January 1965, where it had appeared under a pseudonym ('F. E. Cartus') without any indication of source or of authentication. The very fact of its publication under a pseudonym ought to have put readers on their guard. Mgr Quinn, who is from Chicago, made this prayer his own (in all good faith, one may believe) and spoke about it at an interfaith gathering.

"No bureau of the Vatican can have confirmed the authenticity of this prayer, which exists neither at the Apostolic Penitentiary, nor in the writings, whether printed or not, of Pope John XXIII.

"Mgr Loris Capovilla, the trustee of those writings, denies without hesitation this prayer's authenticity.

"Moreover, a careful examination of the text makes it apparent that, in style and vocabulary, the prayer is alien to the late lamented Pontiff." [3]

Shortly before, the French daily *Le Monde* had published an article entitled "La prière pour les juifs attribuée à Jean XXIII est apocryphe". The article presented as coming from the paper's own Rome correspondent and the date October 26. It began with the words:

"The prayer for the Jews attributed to Pope John XXIII is apocryphal". Such the categorical assertion that we have received from a competent Vatican source.

The rest of the article showed that the *Le Monde* reporter and the author of the piece published in *La Documentation catholique* of November 6 had drawn the same source, in Rome. But *Le Monde* made three "smoothings-over". Instead of a clear heading, it chose an obscure and inexact one; "apocryphal", a rather rare word, signifies: of doubtful authenticity. Instead of mentioning that the text had originated with Commentary, organ of the American Jewish Committee, it was content with saying "[this prayer] has been published in the United States." Finally, to depreciate a bit more what it called "the assertion" (proposition put forth as true) of a competent Vatican source, the newspaper added the following remark:

> This disclaimer concerns quite precisely solely this text. It should hardly call into question the attitude of Pope John who expressed, as is known, his desire to include in the Council's documents a declaration on the Jews the main author of which was Cardinal Bea [4].

1967

Six months after that word of caution from *Le Monde*, Henri Fesquet, its special correspondent in Lyon at the French Congress of Judeo-Christian Friendship, nevertheless began his piece in these terms:

> The epic event of the State of Israel's rebirth, despite the ambiguity of its significance, surpassed the world's expectations whilst the Roman Church gave itself a Pope who was truly attentive to the beseeching of Jules Isaac, author of *L 'Enseignement du mépris* [English title: *The teaching of Contempt: Christian roots of anti-Semitism*]; did John XXIII not admit: "The sign of Cain is etched on our foreheads. Centuries and centuries of blindness have closed our eyes. Forgive us, Lord, for having crucified Thee a second time in the flesh of the Jews. For we knew not what we did"? [5]

Henri Fesquet's version may be compared with the counterfeiters' original.

Some days later, *Le Monde* issued a rectification under the simple heading "Jean XXIII et les juifs". It confided that the bit of the "prayer" quoted by its correspondent had been "taken from Mr P.E. Lapide's book *Rome et les Juifs,* just published - translated from the English [English title: *The Last three Popes and the Jews*] - by the editions du Seuil". After this advertisement for a work containing a forgery, it added that Mgr Capovilla had "belatedly [sic] denied the [prayer's] authenticity [6]".

1974-1975

In its issue dated December 31, 1974, *Le Monde* printed a letter from "Mr Paul Samuel, of Paris" under the heading "L'UNESCO, le Vatican et Israël". It was a protest against the Vatican's award of the John XXIII prize to UNESCO. Mr Samuel considered that UNESCO, in excluding Israel, had obeyed "the dictatorship of oil totalitarianism"; as for the Vatican's decision, he criticised it, deeming that "the greatest Pope of the twentieth century, John XXIII, would not have acted in this way". And he proceeded to quote the text of the "prayer". *Le Monde* agreed to publish this letter although it contained a fake: a fake against which the paper no longer thought it necessary to put its readers on guard [7].

Irony had it that some Jews, probably moved and delighted at discovering the "prayer", should write to the newspaper expressing their surprise at the silence hitherto surrounding that document. Such was the case with "Mr and Mrs Léon Zack of Vanves". It was necessary indeed to resign to issuing a disclaimer. But *Le Monde's* assumed such a form that the reader might believe that the "apocryphal text" had been circulated with the good (or bad) faith by *Commentary* (there being no indication of the review's Jewish character) and "various organs in Europe, including *La Documentation catholique*". The headline chosen was "À propos de la prière apocryphe de Jean XXIII sur les juifs" [8].

1983

In *Le Monde* of January 30, 1983, Alexandre Szombati wrote a purported "Inquiry into the murder of Theodor Erich von Furtenbach who called himself a Nazi". One sentence read:

> After the war, the Church quit the path of error along which it had strayed and a Pope himself acknowledged "the sign of Cain on our foreheads".

Those words were attributed to a "witness" to the murder, a murder which, let it be said in passing, was to earn the perpetrator but a single day in jail; he had done a pious deed [9].

1989

In September of 1989, in a programme on the French television channel *La Cinq* about the Auschwitz Carmelite convent, Jean Kahn, president of the

Conseil représentative des institutions juives de France (CRIF), read aloud John XXIII's "prayer" before the Jesuit theologian Father Martelet, Father Martelet steered clear of pointing out that it was a forgery.

The following month, on the occasion of the Jewish new year, the same Jean Kahn gave an interview to two *Le Monde* reporters, Patrice Jarreau and Henri Tincq, during which he stated:

> [Mgr Decourtray] has decided, also, to send all parishes [of his diocese] a copy of the last prayer composed by John XXIII, regretting the centuries of the Church's contempt for the Jewish people, for it is to be read aloud by the priests [10].

In a brief letter of the following day, a reader of the paper wrote to its managing editor, André Fontaine:

> Jean Kahn of the Conseil représentatif des institutions juives de France (CRIF), has asserted to you (*Le Monde*, October 3, 1989) that Cardinal Decoutray has decided to send "John XXIIl's prayer for the Jews" to all [his] parishes. I am surprised that on this occasion your paper, which printed that statement in an "interview" with Jean Kahn, should not have thought it necessary to recall, as it has done at least once in the past in 1974 or thereabouts, that this prayer is nothing but a fake; you spoke euphemistically at the time of an "apocryphal" text. I await your rectification [11].

The rectification never came and the letter "for publication" was not published. I am unaware whether Cardinal Decourtray ever intended to circulate the bogus prayer or whether that was a project abusively ascribed to him by Jean Kahn. Perhaps the cardinal of Lyon had that inntention and perhaps he even put it into effect. Jean Kahn is a case. He would seem to be endowed with a "particular sensitivity" and with "an extra bit of soul", amongst his coreligionists there seem to exist, in effect, a particular sensitivity that makes a Jewish voter a voter with an extra bit of soul [12]. For him, French Jews are "Frenchmen often more patriotic than the others [13]".

Thus was the daily *Le Monde* following a tradition of its own observed in such cases, to have dealt with the the subject in an oblique manner all throughout the period from 1966 to 1989.

The officials of the American Jewish Committee took part, in their style, in the campaign directed towards the Vatican and Paul VI to have the Catholic Church proceed to unburden the Jews of their responsibility in "the sentencing to death of Jesus Christ". As the reader may recall, texts in the Good Friday service denounce the "perfidious Jews" who had demanded that sentence of Pontius Pilate:

[The Jews] wished to lay all the blame for their crime on the person of the [Roman] judge; but could they fool God, who is also a judge? Pilate was a participant in their crime to the extent of what he did: but, if compared with them, he is to be found much less criminal [14].

In 1965, organised Jewry was hoping that the Vatican II Ecumenical Council would declare unambiguously the non-perfidy of the Jews and their absence of responsibility in Christ's being condemned to death. But, the longer the Council ran on, the more it appeared that the Vatican was hesitating, especially in the face of pressure from the Eastern Catholics.

All told, the "Declaration on the Relation of the Church to Non-Christian Religions (*Nostra AEtate*)" of October 28, 1965 made broad concessions to the Jews but disappointed them.

This is a little-known point and, today, rumour will have it that the Church, in 1965, withdrew the charge of perfidy along with that of any responsibility in Christ's sentencing. The truth is different. The Council remembered "the bond that spiritually ties the people of the New Covenant to Abraham's stock", decried and deplored anti-semitism, said that "Christ underwent His passion and death freely, because of the sins of men and out of infinite love, in order that all may reach salvation". It insisted that "the Jews should not be presented as rejected or accursed by God, as if this followed from the Holy Scriptures".

But some words - eight in the Latin text - recalled all the same, in a concessive clause, that "the Jewish authorities and those who followed their lead pressed for the death of Christ (*auctotitates Judaeorum cum suis asseclis mortem Christi urserunt*). The Council fathers could not, after all, alter the contents of the Gospel account [15].

Jacob Kaplan, chief rabbi of France from 1955 to 1980, whilst expressing his gladness at certain features of the declaration, would write:

> What was hoped of Vatican II was above all a rejection of the charge
> of deicide brought against the Jews. One was entitled to hope for it. As
> is known, there were three projects on the matter. The first in 1963, the
> second in 1964, the last which became definitive in 1965. However, the
> 1964 version (the second) effectively rejected the charge of deicide, but
> in the last one there was no mention of it. It was quite simply eliminated.
> What had happened? An article in *Le Monde* (June 19, 1987) lets us
> know. In the review of a book written in English by an orientalist of some
> authority, Bernard Lewis, a passage of the author's *Sémites et Antisémites*
> [Semites and Anti-semites: an inquiry into conflict and prejudice] is given
> in which he reports on the pressures brought to bear on the Vatican by Arab
> nations in order that the Jews not be exculpated from the crime of deicide.
> The Vatican yielded. Regretting the elimination, Cardinal Liénart of Lyon
> could not help saying: "One might believe that the Council did not wish to
> clear the Jewish people of the charge of deicide" [16].

1990

Today other struggles mobilise the Jews in their demands on the
Catholics.

A recent article in *Le Monde* by Henri Tincq recalls that, in the affair
of the Auschwitz Carmelites, the Jews have obtained satisfaction and the
nuns will have to leave their place of prayer on the edge of the camp for
a centre of dialogue and research on the Shoah [17]. The Catholics have
already laid out large sums of money for the centre's construction but Pope
John Paul II has announced the freeing of an additional $100,000 to speed
up the work.

Still, the Pope remains suspect and, as the *Le Monde* reporter says,
"proceedings for 'revisionism' have been instituted against John Paul II".
The Pope is taking too long to bring out a document that he had, in September
1987, promised to draft on the "Holocaust" and that was to endorse the
notion of the Nazi gas chambers' reality [18]. He is too interested in the project
of Queen Isabella the Catholic's beatification. The Jews, with the support
of Mgr Lustiger, Cardinal of Paris and an ethnic Jew himself, are striving
to prevent the beatification of a "too Catholic" Queen, guilty of having, in

1492, issued the edict banishing the Jews from her realm, a deed done under the influence of Grand Inquisitor Torquemada who, it is said, had abjured his original faith: Judaism.

The myth of "John XXIII's prayer for the Jews" is far from vigorous, but it lingers discreetly and, thanks to that very discretion, it may yet survive for a fair number of years.

As for the American Jewish Committee, still in good stride, it has recently announced two false news items: according to its Paris correspondent (?), Roger Kaplan, the Fabius-Gayssot bill has not been passed and Faurisson is deceased.

Notes to Appendix I

1. *Commentary*, monthly of the American Jewish Committee (New York, Chicago, Los Angeles), January 1965, n° 1, vol. 39, p. 19-29; the "prayer" appears on page 21.
2. *La Documentation catholique*, October 2, 1966, col. 1728.
3. *La Documentation catholique*, November 6, 1966, col. 1908-1909.
4. *Le Monde*, October 27, 1966, p. 9.
5. *Le Monde*, April 21, 1967, p. 11.
6. *Le Monde*, May 7-8,1967, p. 17.
7. *Le Monde*, December 31, 1974, p. 4.
8. *Le Monde*, February 2, 1975, p. 8.
9. *Le Monde*, January 30,1983, supplement, p. I, IV-V. Concerning the individual going by the name of "Szombat", one may read an article that I devoted to him entitled: "Une enquête du Monde diplomatique sur les chambres à gaz (mars 1988)" in the *Annales d'histoire révisionniste*, n° 4, Spring 1988, p. 135-149, reprinted in volume II of my *Écrits révisionnistes, op. cit.*, on pages 751-763.
10. *Le Monde*, October 3, 1989, p. 16.
11. Letter from Mr G. D., kindly conveyed to me by its author.
12. *Le Quotidien de Paris*, February 11, 1986, p. 6.
13. *Le Figaro*, November 20, 1989, p. 16. A piece to be read in parallel with André Glucksmann's "L'Europe sera 'juive' ou ne sera pas" (*Libération*, April 16, 1982, p. 14) and with a statement by chief rabbi Sitruk: "Every French Jew is a representative of Israel" (*Le Monde*, AFP, July 12, 1990, p. 7), a remark that was to be distorted and softened by two *Le Monde* journalists who subsequently asked him: "During your latest trip to Israel, did you not state that every French Jew *had to consider himself* as a representative of Israel?

Le Monde, report by Jean -Michel and Henri Tincq, September 30, 1990, p.9) (my emphasis).

14. (*Le Monde*, report by Jean-Michel Dumay and Henri Tincq, September 30, 1990, p. 9) (my emphasis).

15. Dom Gaspard Lefebvre, *Missel vespéral romain (quotidien)*, 1946 [1920], Good Friday, Tenebrae Service, 6th lesson, p. 674.

16. www.vatican.va/archive/hist_councils/ii_vatican_council/documents/vat-ii_ decl_19651028_nostra-aetate_en.html.

17. "Dossier juifs et catholiques en dialogue", *La Documentation catholique*, July 3, 1988, p. 680.

18. *Le Monde*, December 7, 1990, p. 1, 14.

19. Nonetheless, on August 26, 1989, in a message to Polish bishops, he at last evoked the extermination of the Jews in the gas chambers. Then, on September 27, 1990, *L'Osservatore Romano* published on its front page an article on his general audience of the previous day relating a "meditation of the 'Cycle of Jasna Gora' [Poland]". John Paul II, it read, speaking of the Jews, had stated, in Polish: "This people underwent the terrible death of millions of their sons and daughters. At first they were stigmatised in a particular way. Later, they were pushed into the ghetto in separate neighbourhoods. Then they were taken to the gas-chambers, and put to death - simply because they were children of this people (*Poi portati allé camere a gas, dando loro la morte - soltanto perché erano figli di questo popolo*)". Barring an error on my part, John Paul II will thus have been the first Pope to sanction in that way - timidly, it is true - the existence of the homicidal gas chambers.

APPENDIX II

ACCORDING TO THE TALMUD, JESUS IS PLUNGED FOR ETERNITY IN BOILING HOT EXCREMENT

[March 31,1995]

The Talmud greatly permeates Jewish life, including the material aspects of everyday existence. It is the transcription of the Jewish oral tradition. A fundamental work of Judaism, it is meant to serve as a code of canon law and civil law.

The Jews often complain of their portrayal as given by either the Gospels or Christian doctrine. But what image is to be found, for instance, of Jesus Christ in the Talmud?

That image is an atrocious one. All by itself, the fate reserved for Jesus after his death shows what the Talmudists think of the "false Messiah" for, in a chapter dealing with him and two other sworn enemies of the Jews (the emperor Titus, destroyer of Jerusalem in 70 AD, and the Mesopotamian prophet Balaam, who had cursed the Hebrews at the behest of king Moab), one may read:

[In the first century AD, a certain] Onkelos son of Kolonikos was the son of Titus's sister. He had a mind to convert himself to Judaism. He went and raised Titus from the dead by magical arts, and asked him: Who is most in repute in the [other] world? He replied: Israel. [...] He asked him: What is your punishment [in the other world]? He replied: What I decreed for myself. Every day my ashes are collected and sentence is passed on me and I am burnt and my ashes scattered over the seven seas. He then went and raised Balaam by incantations. He asked him: Who is in repute in the other world? He replied: Israel. [...] He then asked: What is your punishment? He replied: With boiling hot semen. He then went and raised by incantations the sinners of Israel [*or, as stated in a note referring to the Munich codex of the Talmud, Jesus alone*]. He asked them: Who is in repute in the other world? They replied: Israel. What about joining them? They replied: Seek their welfare, seek not their harm. Whoever touches them touches the apple of his eye. He said: What is your punishment? They replied: With boiling hot excrement, since a Master has said: Whoever mocks at the words of the Sages is punished with boiling hot excrement.

SOURCES

1. *Der Babylonische Talmud* [Gittin, V, VI, Fol. 57], neu übertragen durch Lazarus Goldschmidt, Berlin, Jüdischer Verlag, 1932, p. 368 (*"Mit siedendem Kote"*).
2. *The Babylonian Talmud* [Seder Nashim, Gittin, Fol. 57], under the editorship of Rabbi Dr I. Epstein, London, The Soncino Press, 1936, p. 260-261 (*"With boiling hot excrement"*).
PS The German version has Jesus's name appearing in the body of the text itself and the English version in a footnote, n° 4.

Explanation: I drafted this text for the barrister of Marcel Junin, a retired professor in the Catholic education system in France. In a letter to the daily *Sud-Ouest*, Mr Junin had, in moderate terms, expressed his disagreement with Mgr Eyt, Archbishop of Bordeaux, who, in a conference, had stated that the Romans alone were responsible for the death of Jesus. The chief rabbi of Bordeaux intervened to say that the Jews had borne no responsibility in Jesus's death, seeing as the Gospel account was, on that point, riddled with implausibilities. The LICRA ("International league against racism and antisemitism") brought charges against Mr Junin who, in first instance, was acquitted but the LICRA appealed. The appeal was heard in Agen, where the decision will be handed down on June 12. The barrister is pessimistic. [The court of appeal found Mr Junin guilty of incitement to racial or religious hatred, imposing a fine (suspended) and ordering him to pay damages and costs.]

I owe the foregoing texts and references to Arthur Butz. It seems that in its current versions, except those in Hebrew, the Talmud is regularly falsified. See the extraordinary little book by Israel Shahak, *Jewish History, Jewish Religion: The Weight of Three Thousand Years* (London, Boulder [Colorado], Pluto Press, 1994).

APPENDIX III

SIX QUESTIONS TO JOHN PAUL II ABOUT EDITH STEIN

[November 4, 1998]

In St Peter's Square in the Vatican, on Sunday October 11, 1998, Pope John Paul II conducted the canonisation of Teresa Benedicta of the Cross (Edith Stein in her secular life), a Carmelite nun of Jewish origin who was born in Breslau, lower Silesia on October 12, 1891 and who, according to the official version, died at Auschwitz, upper Silesia on August 9, 1942. In the course of his homily the pope stated:

> Because she was Jewish, Edith Stein was taken with her sister Rosa and many other Catholic Jews from the Netherlands to the concentration camp in Auschwitz, where she died with them in the gas chambers[1].

The end of this sentence implies that, for the pope, the Nazi gas chambers did indeed exist. Already in 1989 John Paul II had ventured to evoke, in a message to Polish bishops, "the extermination of the Jews... doomed to the gas chambers"; then in 1990, at an audience where he evoked a "meditation of the 'Cycle of Jasna Gora'", he spoke anew of the "*camere a gas*"[2]. Never until that time had he or any other Pope before him thus taken the responsibility to assert the existence and the functioning of veritable chemical slaughterhouses in a German concentration camp. Pius XII in particular, who died in 1958, had always refrained from doing so and, like his contemporaries Churchill, Eisenhower, and de Gaulle refused to mention either genocide or gas chambers in the war memoirs that they wrote between 1948 and 1959.

Why did John Paul II take this extraordinary initiative, and what evidence did he have at his disposal to assert the existence of those gas chambers, then specify that Edith Stein, her sister Rosa, and numerous other Jews from land had met their deaths in such gas chambers at Auschwitz?

Moreover, John Paul II added in the same homily:

> From now on, as we celebrate the memory of this new saint from year to year, we must also remember the *Shoah,* that cruel plan to exterminate

a people, a plan to which millions of our Jewish brothers and sisters fell victim.

There too, a question arises: what evidence did the pope have, on the one hand, to assert the existence of a programme aiming to eliminate the Jewish people and, on the other hand, to put forth the figure of several million victims of that programme? No historian (and particularly not Raul Hilberg) today dare claim to have found the least trace of such a plan, whether in the "Wannsee Protocol" or anywhere else; as for the millions of Jewish victims, where or when has the breakdown of Jewish losses ever been done?

With these questions and a few others in mind, I have consulted, in the vast bibliography devoted to E. Stein, first a work of reference published in France in 1990, then three recent books which have come out in 1998 and, finally, quite a number of articles in various languages. I am conscious of the fact that this has been a limited inquiry. Naturally, if permission to do so were granted to revisionists, I should consult, first, the extremely rich archives of the International Tracing Service (ITS), located at Arolsen-Waldeck in Germany; unhappily these archives are kept under close supervision, notably at the behest of the State of Israel. The dossier put together with a view to E. Stein's beatification, then her canonisation, would also interest me but the Vatican does not allow such consultation. I am thus reduced to requesting of the Vatican authorities, and of the Pope in particular, the favour of a response to the six questions put forth in my conclusion and to certain others which may be noted in the body of the present text.

From the various publications that I have consulted, it emerges that in reality it is not known where, when, or how E. Stein and her sister died. Thus it seems clear that one cannot rightly state as certain that they were **1)** killed, **2)** in one or more gas chambers at Auschwitz, **3)** on August 1942 (that being the date of death sanctioned by numerous authors as well as by the Pope, who has expressed his desire to make the anniversary of E. Stein's demise a day of commemoration, for the entire Roman Catholic church, of the "Shoah").

The Auschwitz "calendar"

According to the 1989 edition of Danuta Czech's "Auschwitz calendar of events", E. Stein, her sister Rosa, and 985 other Jews were deported from the camp of Westerbork in the Netherlands, arriving at Auschwitz on the 8th (and not the 9th) of August 1942. D. Czech would have her readers believe that of these 987 Jews, 464 were registered for work (315 men and 149 women), whilst the other 523 were immediately gassed [3]. As always in the "calendar", this latter assertion is not supported by any evidence; thus, for that matter, a number of Jews who, as I have been able to show, survived the war are listed by this "calendar" as having been gassed. These 523 persons, of whom D. Czech seems to have found no trace in the camp archives, may well have been set down at Cosel (a stop along the way) or, just as well, been sent directly to one of the sub-camps of the Auschwitz complex, or to any other concentration or labour camp.

According to sister Waltraud Herbstrith's book

In *Das Wahre Gesicht Edith Steins* (published in English under the title *Edith Stein, a biography*), generally considered as a work of reference, sister Waltraud Herbstrith writes:

> The Dutch official state journal of 16 February 1950 carried the names of all of the Jews who had been deported from Holland on 7 August [1942]. In list no. 34 one may read "Number 44074, Edith Theresia Hedwig Stein, born 12 October 1891 in Breslau [Silesia], [transported] from Echt [Netherlands], died 9 August 1942"[4].

And she goes on to add:

> As it was acknowledged legally that no-one from that convoy had survived, 19th of August [1942] was declared the victims' date of decease.

It will be noted that this *official journal* does not specify the date of E. Stein's death and that W. Herbstrith declares that date to be "acknowledged legally" *(gerichtnotorisch feststand)*, all of which implies that no real investigation has ever been earned out; this purported date of decease is lit of speculation, as happens in France with what is known as a *"jugement déclaratif de décès"* (declaratory finding of decease) [5].

According to the French weekly La Vie

A passage in a recent article in La Vie (formerly *La Vie catholique illustrée*) reads as follows:

> [E. Stein was] executed in obscure conditions, doubtless in Auschwitz, officially the 9th of August 1942 [6].

It will be noted that the author of the article acknowledges that the date and place of E. Stein's death are not really known; as for the choice of the word "executed", it is abusive since, as it is unclear where and when her death occurred, it can hardly be known *how* it occurred.

According to the book by Joachim Bouflet

In his *Edith Stein, philosophe crucifiée,* Joachim Bouflet writes:

> [E. Stein was deported] to the East. To Auschwitz where she was to be gassed on arrival, the 9th of August, with her sister Rosa [7].

And adds, in his "chronology":

> 9 August 1942: gassed with her sister Rosa at Auschwitz-Birkenau.

It will be noted that the author (apparently unaware that the Stein's convoy arrived at Auschwitz on the 8th of August and not the 9th) points out, on the faith of one knows not what evidence, that the "gassing" took place at Birkenau; at that date, according to the vulgate, this "gassing" could have occurred either at Auschwitz I or at a Birkenau "farm".

According to the book by Bernard Molter

In *Edith Stein, martyre juive de confession chrétienne,* Bernard Mollor writes:

> On 7 August, the [Dutch] convoy departs. For the East. Then, silence. The great silence of Auschwitz-Birkenau where [E. Stein] is exterminated, probably upon arrival on 9 August [8].

And he adds, in his "Repères biographiques" (important dates):

> Probably on the 9th of August, she is gassed to death at Auschwitz-Birkenau.

One will note that the author who, once again, seems not to know that the convoy arrived at Auschwitz on August 8 rather than August 9, has the honesty to write that it is "probably" on that latter date that E. Stein died. As for the word "exterminated", it is all the more abusive here as such a word can be applied only to a group of persons, not to an individual. In writing: "On 7 August, the convoy departs. For the East. Then, silence", the author has brushed against reality; he ought to have stopped there and not added the next sentence.

According to the book by Christian Feldmann

In *Edith Stein; Jüdin, Philosophin, Ordensfrau* (Edith Stein; Jewess, Philosopher, Nun) German author Christian Feldmann writes:

> According to the information of the Ministry of Justice [*of which country?*], Edith and Rosa Stein were gassed immediately after their arrival at Auschwitz, on 9 August 1942 [9].

According to Bernard Dupuy's study

In a study entitled "Edith Stein dans les griffes de la Gestapo/Précisions nouvelles sur son envoi en déportation" (Edith Stein in the Clutches of the Gestapo / New Information on her Deportation), Bernard Dupuy writes:

> Two hundred forty Catholic Jews [among whom E. and R. Stein], identified, arrested, and deported together would seem to have been sent to the gas chambers just after arriving at Auschwitz-Birkenau on 9 August [10].

The author, who acknowledges his debt to W. Herbstrith's work of reference and to the book by J. Bouflet, has the prudence to put that sentence in the conditional but, unlike those by whom he is inspired, he is imprudent enough to tack on the assertion that all of the Catholic Jews would seem to have been, like E. and R. Stein, gassed on 9 August (for: 8 August).

A Widespread Plagiary?

In short, all of these authors seem to have copied one another, or drawn on the same poor and doubtful source, and each of them, finally, adorns the traditional account with a few inventions of his own.

One may consider the question whether the Pope or his counsellors have not, in turn, merely repeated the same hackneyed story of the fate of E. Stein and the other Jews in her convoy without taking the trouble to verify any of it.

Another Question: May E. Stein have died of Typhus ?

If E. Stein did indeed arrive at Auschwitz in August 1942, may she not have perished in one of the dreadful typhoid epidemics which ravaged the camp at the time? Even the town of Auschwitz was touched by them. A number of Germans, including some SS physicians, died of typhus in the camp.

Another Question: Did any members of the Stein family survive the war?

The Pope in his homily saluted

> the many pilgrims who have come to Rome, particularly the members of the *Stein family* who have wanted to be with us on this joyful occasion.

Admittedly, some members of her family had left Europe in time but others remained, in Breslau for instance. Thus one may read in W. Herbstrith's book:

> On 28 July [1942] there came [to E. Stein's knowledge] the terrible news that Edith Stein's brothers and sisters in Breslau, the family of her brother Paul, and her sister Freida had been taken to Theresienstadt [11].

It would be interesting to know the fate of these persons. Did any of them survive the war? If so, were any of their children, born after the war, in attendance at the ceremony?

Were the Dutch bishops primarily responsible
for this deportation?

We are often told that the occupying power cynically deceived the Catholic bishops of the Netherlands: that after having assured them that converted Jews would not be affected by any coercive measures, the Germans, suddenly going back on their word, decided to deport such Jews. But is the truth perhaps altogether different? Did the Dutch Roman Catholic Church perhaps first break its explicit or implicit commitments, then adopt a resolutely provocative attitude towards the occupying forces?

To reply to this grave question, let us compare passages in two of the biographies, referring first to words in C. Feldmann's book which express the anti-German point of view, then to an extract of a document in the book by W. Herbstrith, which shows the German wartime point of view.

C. Feldmann writes:

On 11 July 1942, the spiritual leaders of all [Christian] denominations sent a telegram to the Commissar of the Reich, Seyss-Inquart, in which they protested against the deportation of Jewish families. - To fool everyone, the authorities of the Reich had given assurances that converted Jews were not to be affected by coercive measures. But that did not deter the Churches of the Netherlands from declaring their solidarity with the persecuted Jews. A heated protest against the deportation of Jewish families was read out on 26 July in all the churches of Holland, of all denominations. In the Catholic churches, a pastoral letter asking that all believers make a self-criticism was read out in addition to the protestation: " [...] Have we not nourished feelings of impious hatred and bitterness?" The letter ended with a prayer which was quite provocative in regard to the occupying forces [...]. Such outspoken resistance to the cowing of public conscience could obviously not be tolerated. Still less so as the clergy had violated Reich Commissar Seyss-Inquart's express prohibition of the reading out in church of the protest telegram which had been addressed to him. The Nazi occupying authorities reacted violently on 2 August [...]. They arrested all Catholic Jews, priests and nuns included, 1,200 persons all told, according to some estimates [12].

The reader may note that, even in the eyes of an author very favourable to the cause of the Jews and Catholics, the attitude which the bishops had adopted, in this particular case, was a deliberately provocative one. "A heated protest... a prayer which was quite provocative... Such outspoken resistance... the clergy had violated Reich Commissar Seyss-Inquart's express prohibition": such are the words chosen by C. Feldmann. But there is another point, appreciably more important, which deserves to be stressed and which raises another question: how is it that the Germans arrested the Catholic Jews without at the same time arresting the Protestant ones? How is this difference of reaction to be explained? Is there not a precise reason for this anomaly?

The answer to these questions seems to lie in a German document which C. Feldmann passes over in silence and which W. Herbstrith, unfortunately, cites only in part. It emerges from this document that, for the Germans, the Catholic Church and the various Protestant denominations had been advised that they could intervene in favour of their brethren of Jewish descent but not in favour of unconverted Jews. If these churches looked after their flocks, the Germans would not take action against those among them who were of Jewish blood. A key passage reads:

> The Protestant authorities are not averse to this way of seeing things and have not, for their part, incited any [such] demonstration or prayer in their churches. On the contrary, the Catholic Church, this past Sunday, spoke during its services of the deportation of the Jews. This, according to its leaders, was due to the fact that the Reich Commissar's point of view had not become known everywhere in time [13].

It can be seen there that, from the German authorities' standpoint, the Catholic Church had feigned ignorance of a warning, a promise, and an express prohibition which the Protestant churches, for their part, had heeded. It may well be that, in some Protestant houses of worship, the hierarchy's instructions were at times disregarded but it was the Catholic Church which, at the highest national level, chose not to take heed in the least of the occupying authorities' warning, promise, and express prohibition; it even added to its refusal an act of defiance: it had the protest telegram read out in public, along with the pastoral letter.

That being the case, can it not reasonably be said that it was this refusal to heed, this defiance on the part of the Church, which prompted Edith Stein's deportation? One may deem the Dutch Catholic Church's initiative courageous, just as one may consider bombings and assassinations, carried out by terrorists or resistance fighters, to be justified but, come the time for reprisals - inevitable in the case at hand, according to C. Feldmann himself - where are those who are primarily responsible to be found? Would not E. Stein, R. Stein, and the other Catholic Jews have been spared a deportation which, for some, resulted in death, if the Dutch Catholic Church had behaved in the same way as the Protestant churches? Without meaning to offend anybody, may one not rightfully pose that question?

Why are there such discrepancies between the various translations of the homily?

The Vatican and its official daily newspaper *I'Osservatore Romano* are known for the great care they take in rendering papal documents into various languages. They have no shortage of expert translators. Yet, after a comparison of the different versions (English, French, German, and Italian) of the 11 October homily, two questions arise:

1) How is it that a passage in the German and English versions relates that Edith and Rosa Stein were deported along with "many other *Catholic* Jews from the Netherlands" whereas, in the French and Italian versions, the word "Catholic" does not appear in the corresponding sentence?
2) Why is the French version hebraised in the sense that, whereas the others mention the Lord ("der Herr" "il Signore"), it instead speaks of *Yahvé?*

Conclusion

Through the agency of *l'Osservatore Romano*, to which I address the present text in order that it be passed on to the proper authority in the Vatican, I hereby take the liberty, in summing up, of asking the following questions of John Paul II, in the hope of receiving a reply which I may, with his permission, duly make public:

1. What evidence have you that may establish the death of Edith Stein in an execution gas chamber at Auschwitz on 9 August 1942?

2. What evidence have you of the existence of a German government plan for the physical elimination of the Jewish people?

3. Have you ordered an investigation, particularly in conjunction with the International Tracing Service (ITS) at Arolsen-Waldeck, to determine whether, for example, Edith and Rosa Stein did not die elsewhere than at Auschwitz or did not fall victim to the typhus epidemics which, notably in 1942, ravaged the Auschwitz camp to the point of causing hundreds of deaths per day, sparing neither German guards nor SS camp physicians?

4. Did any members of the Stein family who were interned by the Germans survive the war, and, if so, were any such relatives present at the canonisation ceremony at the Vatican on 11 October 1998?

5. Does the primary responsibility for the German decision to deport the Catholic Jews of the Netherlands not lie with the country's wartime Roman Catholic bishops who, unlike the Protestant authorities, seem to have inspired - or at least knowingly allowed - actions which were likely to prompt such a decision?

6. Why are there such serious discrepancies between the various translations of the homily that you pronounced on 11 October 1998?

NB: The young French historian Vincent Reynouard has recently published a revisionist examination of the case of Edith Stein; see "Sur Edith Stein", *ANEC Informations*, 29 October, 1998, p. 3-5.

Notes to Appendix III

1. *L'Osservatore Romano*, weekly English language edition, 14 October 1998, p.l.

2. *L'Osservatore Romano*, September 27, 1990. See above, p. 78, n 18

3. Danuta Czech, *Kalendarium der Ereignisse im Konzentrationslager Auschwitz-Birkenau 1939-1945*, Rowohlt, Hamburg, 1989, p. 269.

4. Waltraud Herbstrith, *Das Wahre Gesicht Edith Steins* (The True Face of Edith Stein), Kaffke-Verlag, Aschaffenburg, 1987 [1971], verbesserte Auflage [revised and corrected edition], p. 176. (Work published in English translation under the title *Edith Stein, a biography*, Ignatius Press, San Francisco, 1992 [1985].)

5. When the date of a deportee's death is not known, the registry office holds it to be the date on which that person is ascertained or presumed to have arrived in a given camp. In certain Jewish cemeteries in Germany there are headstones bearing mention, in their inscriptions, of the same date of death and the same camp for two or three family members; thus the observer is led to believe that these persons were simultaneously murdered in one particular camp, whereas in reality they may well have perished separately, i.e. on different dates, of different causes, in different circumstances, even in different camps.

6. Jean-Pierre Manigne, "Edith Stein, juive et martyre", *La Vie*, 8 October 1998, p. 71.

7. Joachim Bouflet, *Edith Stein, philosophe crucifiée*, Presses de la Renaissance, Paris, 1998, p. 273.

8. Bernard Molter, *Edith Stein, martyre juive de confession chrétienne*, Cana, Paris, 1998, p. 145.

9. Christian Feldmann, *Edith Stein: juive, athée, moniale* (Edith Stein: Jewess, Atheist, Nun; French translation by Yvan Mudry of *Edith Stein; Jüdin, Philosophin, Ordensfrau* [Edith Stein: Jewess, Philosopher, Nun], Herder, Freiburg, 1987), Saint-Augustin, Paris, 1998, p. 144.

10. Bernard Dupuy, "Edith Stein dans les griffes de la Gestapo / Précisions nouvelles sur son envoi en déportation", *Istina* (Paris) no. XLIII (1998), p. 289.

11. Waltraud Herbstrith, *op. cit.*, p. 165.

12. Christian Feldmann, *op. cit.*, p. 138-139

13. Waltraud Herbstrith, *op. cit.* ,p. 177.

APPENDIX IV

LETTER FROM HENRI ROQUES TO HENRI AMOUROUX

Sir,

I have read with interest your article entitled "Le cinéma trahit-il'histoire?" (Does the cinema betray history?) *Figaro-Magazine* of February 23, 2002).

You put the question, but I have no doubt that your answer is affirmative. Moreover, further on you write: "History is not written with a film." That sentence holds for a fair number of other cinematic productions, notably *Holocaust*, a pure Hollywood-style serial, and Claude Lanzmann's *Shoah*, to stay with the same subject matter. I appreciate your defence of Pope Pius XII and of the Catholic Church as a whole. I should like, nonetheless, to draw your attention to the figure of Kurt Gerstein.

You were shocked, and rightly so, at the transformation of the awful Joseph Joanovici into a near-hero of the Resistance in a recent television film. You were quite right to recall that he was a racketeer protected by the Gestapo who, in 1944, tried to clear his name with the help of an immense ill-gotten fortune. Of course I shall not compare Gerstein to the strange "Mister Joseph". Gerstein was not venal, having come from a comfortable background. His object was to make himself interesting to those around him, gaining their sympathy and complicity with gifts, dazzling them with his winning way; in short, he was consumed with an ambition to play a role, whatever it might be, and his country's defeat provided him with the occasion to stand in the role of which you are aware. The turning of this known psychopath into "God's spy", carrying out his mission in the world by denouncing the gassings at the Belzec camp in August 1942, has something of a sinister hoax about it.

Before saying anything about Gerstein, it seems obvious to me that one must first of all read what he wrote in his "report that became famous", as you yourself term it. That was the reason for the doctoral thesis that I presented at the University of Nantes on June 15, 1985; that thesis if raised a general political and media outcry. I went to see you in person, in 1984 or '85, to give you a copy. I do not know whether you have read it. In my conclusions, I brought up the appraisal of a physician who had been a colleague of Gerstein's at the Waffen SS Institute of Hygiene. He spoke of the instances of "absent mindedness" and the "strange reactions" of that odd SS officer who was unfit for armed service, what with his grave physical and cerebral disorders (he was subject to falling into a pre-comatose state provoked by diabetes). Léon Poliakov himself, who in 1951 revealed Gerstein's testimony in his book *Bréviaire de la haine* [English title: *Harvest of Hate*], was to write in 1967: "Psychiatrists would have a good deal to tell us about the Gerstein case." I shall not go into the staggering implausibilities that I brought to the fore in my dissertation. If you find your copy of it you will be able to acquaint yourself with them. I want only to tell you that you yourself were misled in writing that he was "given the task to go observe at Belzec (and not Belzen) and Treblinka, two concentration camps, the testing of Zyklon B on deportees." In none of the six versions of his "Confessions" does Gerstein speak of Zyklon B. It was a product that he knew well, since he was in charge of supplying the camps with it for use as a disinfectant. He tells an outrageous story of hydrogen cyanide contained in 45 steel bottles. That liquid or gaseous substance could therefore not be Zyklon B, a solid stored in metal cans. Gerstein claims to have concealed those bottles before arriving at the Belzec camp with the help of a chauffeur whom he did not know but whom he suspected of belonging to the secret service of the SS (sic).

Gerstein then tells of an alleged gassing by the emissions of a Diesel engine. We are very far, as you may see, from tests with Zyklon B. Nothing of what Gerstein recounts holds up; he speaks indifferently of hydrogen cyanide and of potassium cyanide as if they were the same thing. However, there is as much difference between the two as between hydrochloric acid and sodium chloride (table salt).

As for Gerstein's behaviour, it is very dubious. I met his widow in 1983. She herself, although quite anxious to defend her husband, told me that he had at his disposal a budget for making the necessary purchases for disinfection and that he used it to buy items of food rare in wartime. Pierre Joffroy, Gerstein's great hagiographer, makes an analogous remark in his book (*L'Espion de Dieu*, Seghers, 1992 [1969], p. 186 [English edition: *A spy for God: the ordeal of Kurt Gerstein*, Collins, London, 1971): he writes that, according to his wife, the real reason for Gerstein's distress or panic in

Berlin in 1942 may well have been his dread at the approach of the hygiene institute's year-end verification of expenditures.

I talked with an Alsatian gentleman who had had Gerstein as his chief at the Berlin institute. When 17 or 18 years old, he was twice sent on a very special mission to Paris; he was assigned with making purchases of kitchen oil (!) in a Jewish neighbourhood there. Finally, I have discovered on the website of the *Encyclopaedia Universalis* quite a curious bit of information. How did a painting by Matisse find its way to the Gerstein home? Discreetly, the article is content with mentioning "unknown circumstances".

The idealised image of Gerstein as "God's spy" on a mission "behind the scenes in the centre of evil" thus finds itself seriously tarnished, even called into doubt altogether. To give historical standing to this top-flight lunatic is to take advantage of human naivety. The historian's role is to limit damage, to take on false ideas and to get as near to the truth as possible.

Pius XII never received any Gerstein report. Besides, had he ever held in his hands such a preposterous text, the product of a sick brain, he would not have taken any account of it. Speaking out against the absurd character of Gerstein's testimony is the best way to defend Pius XII and the Catholic Church, both attacked by a scandalous film.

I have great regard for your intellectual honesty as a historian. That is why I should appreciate a reply on your part.

Yours respectfully,

Henri Roques, March 18, 2002

NB: The key to the Gerstein mystery is perhaps to be found in an article at the website www.universalis.fr devoted to the Nazis' despoiling of artwork (p.7): "Henri Matisse - *Paysage, le mur rose.* All trace was lost of this 'Pink wall of Calvi hospital' painted by Matisse in 1897. [...] It was found again, in July 1947, at Tübingen, in the cache of an SS officer, Kurt Gerstein [...]." That article is reserved for the site's subscribers. On February 23, 2003 Didier Schulmann, curator at the national museum of modern art in Paris, and Florent Brayard, researcher at the *Institut d'histoire du Temps présent*, dealt with the matter of "Henri Matisse's *Le mur rose (de I'hôpital d'jaccio*[sic]), 1898, discovered, in Germany in 1948, in a cache of the

SS officer Kurt Gerstein"

Index of names mentioned

9 780906 879245